Framework FOCUS

Writing

Christine Davies
Darren Latchford

Published by Letts Educational
The Chiswick Centre
414 Chiswick High Road
London W4 5TF

t 020 89963333

f 020 87428390

e mail@lettsed.co.uk

w www.letts-education.com

Letts Educational Limited is a division of Granada Learning Limited, part of Granada plc.

First published 2002

ISBN 1840857072

British Library Cataloguing in Publication Data
A catalogue record for this book is available from the British Library.

Developed and packaged by McLean Press Ltd

Commissioned by Helen Clark

Project management by Vicky Butt

Edited by Debbie Seymour

Cover design by bigtop, Bicester, UK

Internal design by bigtop, Bicester, UK

Acknowledgements

The publishers would like to thank the following for permission to use copyright material. Every effort has been made to trace copyright holders and to obtain their permission for the use of copyright material. The authors and publishers will gladly receive information enabling them to rectify any error or omission in subsequent editions.

BBC Worldwide page 40, Faber & Faber pages 48, 49, 53, Penguin UK page 45, Peters Fraser & Dunlop page 54.

Illustrations by James Arnold, Paul McCaffrey, Linda Combi and Darren Lingard

Production by PDQ

Printed and bound in the UK by Ashford Colour Press

Contents

Structuring stories (1)

Aims

- To investigate how stories are structured: with an arresting opening, a developing plot, a complication, a crisis and a satisfying resolution.

Starter session

Look at these famous opening lines.

Pre 1914

'Was she beautiful or not beautiful?'

Daniel Deronda, George Eliot

'1801. I have just returned from a visit to my landlord – the solitary neighbour that I shall be troubled with.'

Wuthering Heights, Emily Brontë

'Marley was dead, to begin with. There is no doubt whatever about that.'

A Christmas Carol, Charles Dickens

Post 1914

'Mr and Mrs Dursley, of number four, Privet Drive, were proud to say that they were perfectly normal, thank you very much.'

Harry Potter and the Philosopher's Stone, J.K. Rowling

'Last night I dreamt I went to Manderley again.'

Rebecca, Daphne du Maurier

'The tropical rain fell in drenching sheets, hammering the corrugated roof of the clinic building, roaring down the metal gutters, splashing on the ground in a torrent.'

Jurassic Park, Michael Crighton

Pick a favourite, and give your teacher three reasons why your chosen lines make you want to read the rest of the story.

Introduction

Most stories follow a recognisable **structure**. Look at the flowchart below.

Opening – The first few lines set the scene for the rest of the story. They must grab the reader's attention and make them want to read on.

Development of plot – Moving on from the opening, the reader is given more information about the characters, the setting and the action of the plot. The development section answers the question: 'What happens next?'.

Complication – Many plots involve some sort of central problem, introduced at this point, for the main character to tackle.

Crisis – This is the climax of the story. The plot has been developing to reach this crucial point.

Resolution – The end of the story resolves the crisis and concludes the plot.

1 Now read this very short story (Text 1) by Franz Kafka. Identify all five structural features.

A LITTLE FABLE

'Alas,' said the mouse, 'the whole world is growing smaller every day. At the beginning it was so big I was afraid, I kept running and running, and I was glad when I saw walls far away to the right and left, but these long walls have narrowed so quickly that I am in the last chamber already, and there in the corner stands the trap that I must run into.' 'You only need to change your direction,' said the cat, and ate it up.

Development

Here is the opening paragraph of a story called **'Metamorphosis'** (Text 2), also by Franz Kafka.

1 Read it by yourself, and then, in groups, discuss how effective it is as the start of a story.

 TEXT **2**

METAMORPHOSIS (extract)

When Gregor Samsa awoke one morning from troubled dreams he found himself transformed in his bed into a monstrous insect. He was lying on his hard shell-like back and by lifting his head a little he could see his curved brown belly, divided by stiff arching ribs, on top of which the bed-quilt was precariously poised and seemed about to slide off completely. His numerous legs, which were pathetically thin compared to the rest of his bulk, danced helplessly before his eyes.

2 You are going to develop the plot. What happens to Gregor next? In pairs, brainstorm ideas about the following:

- The practicalities of being a beetle (e.g. no hands, different senses)
- The impact of being a beetle on Gregor's normal day (e.g. breakfast, get washed, get dressed, go to school)
- The effect Gregor has on other people (e.g. his family, his classmates).

3 Feedback your ideas to the class. Your teacher will collect the best ones on the board.

4 Now, using the ideas from the board, write one paragraph to follow on from the opening of 'Metamorphosis'. Remember to:

- Decide what happens next – you only have one paragraph so you need to be focused.
- Make your descriptions vivid – use a variety of adjectives, adverbs, etc.

Review

A film is another kind of story. Think of some gripping openings of films that impressed you. What do you remember? Why did they impress you? Share your ideas with the class.

YEAR 7 · **UNIT 2**

Structuring stories (2)

Aims

- To continue to investigate how stories are structured.
- To look at some endings of novels and work on a complication, a crisis and a resolution to produce a story.

Starter session

Look at these examples of closing lines.

Pre 1914

'Upon the bed, before that whole company, there lay a nearly liquid mass of loathsome – of detestable putridity.'

The Case of M. Valdemar, Edgar Allen Poe

The Time Traveller vanished 3 years ago. And, as everybody knows, he has never returned.'

The Time Machine, H.G. Wells

But, in spite of these deficiencies, the wishes, the hopes, the confidence, the predictions of the small band of true friends who witnessed the ceremony, were fully answered in the perfect happiness of the union.'

Emma, Jane Austen

Post 1914

'So Lyra and her daemon turned away from the world they were born in, and looked towards the sun, and walked into the sky.'

Northern Lights, Philip Pullman

'There was a point to this story, but it has temporarily escaped the chronicler's mind.'

So Long and Thanks for all the Fish, Douglas Adams

'If one domino falls, it will always knock over the next one. The proof by induction is complete.'

Fermat's Last Theorem, Dava Sobel

Can you guess which type of story each ending comes from? Collect your ideas on the board.

Introduction

In this Unit, you are going to complete the story of Gregor, who has turned unexpectedly into a beetle (see Unit 1). Turn back to page 5 and, as a class, remind yourselves of the five structural features your story is going to cover. You have already completed the first two points on the flowchart.

Development

1 You are going to bring the story through a complication, to a crisis and to a final resolution. The outline for each of these three points is given below. However, the details are left for you to decide.

In pairs, brainstorm ideas about the following:

- **The complication** – Gregor starts to change again:
  a What animal does he change into?
  b Does he change entirely, or is he a beetle with a rabbit's tail?
  c Is the change sudden?

- **The crisis** – Whatever Gregor has changed into, a predator arrives which could eat him:
  a Will there be a battle?
  b Will Gregor have to hide or run?
  c The pace of your story needs to move swiftly at this point. Once you have selected a predator, think of some verbs which will create a sense of pace.

- **The resolution:**
  a Who wins: Gregor or the predator?
  b Remember that you will need a clever final sentence.

2 By yourself, collect your ideas in note form. Group them under headings outlined above. Remember that you will only be producing one paragraph for each point – so stay focused.

3 Use your notes to create a draft version of your final three paragraphs. They do not need to be all the same length.

4 You are going to proofread your draft paragraphs. This means reading them through carefully, checking that everything is correct and making any changes required. You could start by checking for the following:

- Correct spelling – use a dictionary to help you
- Correct punctuation – look in particular at any direct speech
- Do you want to make any refinements? – look at your final sentence, your vocabulary, etc.

5 Write a final draft of your story.

Review

Think again of that other type of story, the film. Suggest some exciting or moving endings of films that you have seen. Do you and your friends agree? If so, why; if not, why not?

Creating characters

Aims

- To look at how to portray characters, directly and indirectly, through description, dialogue and action.

Starter session

Look at the table below, with some brief information about four characters. Try and imagine what they might look like and how they might behave.

Name	Age	Likes	Dislikes
Tom Pritchard	12	Gaming; Nu-metal	Sport; homework
Sarah Parsons	14	Films; reading novels	Stupid people; soaps
Robert Fryer	36	Golf; cooking	Politics; loud music
Annabel Willis	42	Rock climbing; skiing	Loud men; package holidays

In pairs, brainstorm as many words as you can to describe what each person is like.

Introduction

Now work on your own. Choose one of the people and imagine that he or she is a character in a story you are writing. Using the **adjectives** and **adverbs** from your brainstorm and any other ideas you have, write a description of him or her. Give your character a name of your own if you want, but make sure it suits his or her personality.

Development

Writers use description, dialogue and action to show what a character is like.

Description – shows what a character is like in terms of their physical appearance and personality. It uses adverbs and adjectives as you did in the Introduction exercise.

Action – shows what a character does and also *how* it is done. For example, if an author writes: 'Jake stopped to help the old lady across the road, even though he knew it would probably mean that he would miss the bus', we know that we are probably meant to like the character of Jake.

On the other hand, if we read: 'Yasmin aimed a kick at the puppy and then spat on the pavement', we know that Yasmin is unlikely to turn out to be the hero of the story.

The writer has shown us what these characters are like without describing what they look like at all.

Dialogue – shows what a character says and also *how* it is said.

1 Read more descriptions of two characters on their way to school.

TEXT **1**

The two Year 7 boys scurried out of the way as Andrea stomped through the school gates. The bell had already gone but she didn't hurry as she crushed her cigarette beneath her six inch, definitely-not-school-uniform, heel. She picked up a stone and threw it idly in the direction of the staff room window. Smiling at the sounds of crashing glass and squealing teachers, she flicked her pink hair out of her eyes and strode towards the door.

TEXT **2**

Richard's heart was beating anxiously as he arrived at the school gate. Late again. He was beginning to wish he hadn't stopped to help Mrs Pollard find her baby's teddy. He straightened his tie and glanced nervously towards the staff room. Hoisting his heavy bag of books on his shoulder, he made a desperate dash for the door, hoping he would make it to the classroom before Miss Bennett arrived to take the register.

2 Working on your own, copy out the words which give a powerful impression of what each person is like.

3 In pairs, discuss the words and phrases you have copied. What impression of each of these characters is created?

4 Now write your own paragraph about a character arriving at school. You could choose:

- Someone who is very fashionable
- Someone who is very popular
- Someone who likes to be alone
- Someone who loves football
- Your own choice of person.

Try to include:

a A description of what he or she looks like

b An account of what they do, what they say and how they say it. Use the hints below for guidance.

5 Share your paragraph in pairs. See if your partner can find examples of the three ways in which you have shown what your character is like:

- Description
- Action
- Dialogue

6 Try to suggest ways in which each person's work could be improved. Now re-write your description, taking notice of these suggestions.

HINTS!

Description
The first part of your paragraph should describe the physical appearance of your character. Make a list of words and phrases to describe what he or she looks like. Remember to use imaginative adjectives and adverbs.

Action
Now make your character perform an action. Remember that it should suit his or her personality.

Dialogue
Next, your character is going to meet someone else and have a short conversation. Think of some of the words you could use instead of 'said' to show exactly what your character is like.

Review

Your teacher will ask a few of you to read your finished paragraphs out to the class. Discuss how effective each paragraph is at presenting character.

The Pied Piper

Aims

- To experiment with creating visual and sound effects in our own writing.
- To investigate the links between the poetry we read and our own writing.

Starter session

As a class, brainstorm words to describe the following:
- A siren (e.g. wail) ● A sneeze (e.g. splat) ● The wind (e.g. swoosh)
- An old car (e.g. judder) ● A crowd (e.g. roar).

Introduction

Here is an extract from **'The Pied Piper of Hamelin'** (Text 1) by Robert Browning. In this poem the Pied Piper, a mysterious character dressed in red and yellow who can charm creatures with his pipe, agrees to rid the town of Hamelin in Germany of its infestation of rats. Here is the part of the poem where the Piper leads the rats away:

1 Read the poem out loud. You could either read one line per person, or divide into two groups and read alternate lines.

2 The rhyme and the rhythm, which you will have noticed when you did your reading of the poem, are two ways in which the writer emphasises how many rats there are. Can you find any other ways he does this?

3 Make notes about the poem under the following headings:
- Rhythm ● Rhyme ● Repetition ● Visual effects
- Sound effects described by the language (e.g. the pipe)
- Sound effects created by the language ● Lists
- Similes ● Punctuation.

Use the hints box to help you.

THE PIED PIPER OF HAMLIN (extract)

Into the street the Piper stept,
    Smiling first a little smile,
As if he knew what magic slept
    In his quiet pipe the while;
Then, like a musical adept,
To blow his pipe his lips he wrinkled,
And green and blue his sharp eyes twinkled
Like a candle-flame where salt is sprinkled;
And ere three shrill notes the pipe uttered,
You heard as if an army muttered;
And the muttering grew to a grumbling;
And the grumbling grew to a mighty rumbling;
And out of the houses the rats came tumbling.
Great rats, small rats, lean rats, brawny rats,
Brown rats, black rats, grey rats, tawny rats,
Grave old plodders, gay young friskers,
    Fathers, mothers, uncles, cousins,
Cocking tails and pricking whiskers'
    Families by tens and dozens,
Brothers, sisters, husbands wives –
Followed the Piper for their lives.

HINTS!

You will have noticed that Robert Browning uses many **short words** to keep the rhythm fast. Think of as many short words as you can to use in your description. For example, if you are describing spectators at a match, your list could start like this: blue, red, hats, scarves, faces, boots, feet…

Browning also uses a **variety of verbs**. Make a list of useful words. For example: clapping, shouting, stamping, screaming…

He also uses **lists** and **repeats** words that are important ('rats' for example). Which word or words could be repeated in your poem?

Think about the **sounds** that your subject will make. You will need to include these sounds in your poem, and also try to create sound effects with your words.

Development

1 You are going to write a poem of your own where you describe crowds of people or large groups of animals. Pick one of the following:
   ● Spectators at a football match or other sporting event
   ● Herds of stampeding animals
   ● Students rushing to leave school at the end of the day
   ● Your own choice of subject.

2 Now write the title of your poem, with each letter starting a new line. Do it like this:

F
O
O
T
B
A
L
L

C
R
O
W
D

Each letter suggests the first word of each line. You are now ready to write a first copy of your poem.

3 When you have finished writing, share your poem with a partner and discuss the effectiveness of your rhythm, vocabulary and sound effects. Make any alterations you want to make to your poem.

4 Write out your poem neatly and illustrate it for a wall display. As you do so, think about the points in the chart below.

5 When you have completed your final draft, fill in this evaluation chart for your own work.

My poem	Marks out of 10
Handwriting – legibility	
Spelling	
Punctuation	
Neat heading	

Review

Look at these lines from **'The Falls of Lodore'** (Text 2) by Robert Southey. He wrote it for his children after they had visited the Falls in the Lake District. He makes his description a long list of participles, the -ing form of the verb:

TEXT **2**

THE FALLS OF LODORE (extract)

'How does the Water
Come down at Lodore?'
My little boy asked me [...]
Advancing and prancing and glancing and dancing,
Recoiling, turmoiling and toiling and boiling,
And gleaming and streaming and steaming and beaming,
And rushing and flushing and brushing and gushing,
And [...]

Put up your hand and suggest some more participles that would describe the water. There are lots more in the poem!

A *pet's poster*

Aims

- To look at writing that gives us information.
- To consider the features of information writing and discover how to organise material in appropriate ways.

Starter session

Let's check we know what 'information' means.

On a piece of paper, make a spider diagram showing the ways in which written information comes to you. Put yourself in the centre and the sources of information (such as encyclopaedias, Internet, leaflet, travel brochure etc) around the edge.

Introduction

Working in teams, compare your diagrams showing sources of information. Your teacher will then build up, on the board, a longer list of these sources. Anything you missed? Why?
Now let's start thinking about *how* information writing works.

INFORMATION

Information gives us **facts** that need to be clear and well ordered.
You can present these as:
- Bullet points (for a short outline), or
- In paragraphs (one key point in each).

You may need **connectives** (joining words and phrases) to link the paragraphs and sequence the ideas clearly.
You may **arrange** by:
- **Chronology** (i.e. by time) with dates in ascending or descending order – for example, an outline of the Second World War with dates
- **Priority** (i.e. by the relative importance of ideas) so that you put the key points first or highlight them – for example, a leaflet warning about the dangers of gas in the home

- **Comparison** to provide information showing similarities or differences – for example, a report on the qualities of two similar cars of different makes.

When presenting information it is useful to remember that:
- Clear, **plain sentences** are probably best for information.
- **Style** depends on the intended audience.
- **Key details** need to be given emphasis.
- In an information poster or leaflet, size and style of **font** are important.
- **Colour** is effective, too.
- **Diagrams**, graphs, facts and figures can be useful.

1 Discuss, as a class, which of the above ideas are most important in putting across information.

2 Can you think of a good example of information writing you have seen? What did you like about it and why do you remember it?

Development

You are going to compose a piece of information writing about choosing a pet.

- This will be a leaflet (one or two sides of A4 paper) about a domestic pet. It will be displayed at the vet's, at the library and in RSPCA rescue homes.
- Its audience is young people of your own age.
- It will help them in their choice of a pet.
- It will give them useful and lively information about the creature.

1 What information do you think the leaflet should include? The leaflet may include some of these ideas:
- What the pet eats ● The equipment you need to care for it
- How it lives ● What it needs to enjoy life
- The pleasures it will give you ● The difficulties it creates
- Health care problems ● The various breeds.

2 What do you think you might need to do to get your poster noticed? How could you design it? You will need:
- A bold heading (naming the pet)
- Some illustrations
- About six main points written up as six short paragraphs
- Each paragraph will deal with a key point.

3 Now let's start to plan this leaflet.

- Let's think about the pleasures and the difficulties of having a pet (this will give you two of your six paragraphs).
- Write down points on each.
- Read them to a partner and listen to his or her comments.
- In the light of your discussion do you want to change, add to or remove any of your points?

4 Now plan, on your own, the other four paragraphs.

- What are you going to choose from the list of ideas above?
- Think about **priority**: which points go first or are given most space?
- Experiment with **presentation**: for lists within a paragraph (of food or equipment, for example), you may prefer to use bullet points.

You should now have notes for your six paragraphs.

5 When your plan is complete, make a fair copy, check it and make any last-minute revisions.

6 Now you are going to make the leaflet itself.

- Remember the eye-catching **headings**, and add one or two illustrations.
- If you work in ICT, scan in photos or find **pictures** on the Internet.
- The **style** can be quite colloquial to appeal to the young reader.
- **Proofread** the text and check the presentation.

Review

As a class, go over what you have learned about information writing and how it is constructed. Which source of information writing do you find most memorable:

- Internet
- Street poster
- Catalogue
- Specialist magazine
- Book?

Explaining the water cycle

Aims

- To look at writing that explains something to us. We will be thinking about how to explain a process logically and how to link cause and effect.

Starter session

Let's think about the differences between '**to instruct**' and '**to explain**'. Do they mean the same thing? Does their meaning overlap? Is there any ambiguity?

- Put up your hands and tell your classmates about your ideas.
- When you have reached clear conclusions, write the two definitions into your exercise book.
- Discuss briefly with a partner where you would see writing to instruct in your school. In which school subjects would you use writing to explain?

Introduction

Now let's consider what makes a good explanation.

INFORMATION

- A good explanation is clear and well structured.
- We are not concerned here with our feelings or atmospheric description. We just want to know **how** or **why** something happens.

Here are some features of explanatory writing to notice and to use:

- It has a clear **structure** of paragraphs.
- Each paragraph deals with a **key idea**.
- The ideas are in **logical order**, taking us from cause to effect.
- **Connectives**, especially to start paragraphs, help link ideas and move forward.
- It is often (but not always, as in history writing) written in the **present tense**.

- It does not use the familiar personal style of 'I' or 'we' (first person pronouns). It tends to use **second person** (you) or **third person** (he, she, it, they) pronouns and to be more **impersonal**.
- The **passive mood** of verbs is sometimes used.
- **Diagrams or illustrations** are sometimes used to support the writing.

Connectives are words or short phrases that link ideas:
also, however, on the other hand, by contrast, besides, for example, firstly, secondly, thirdly, finally, therefore, meanwhile etc

Passives
'The wheel is turned by...'
'The lava is pushed from the volcano...'

Development

1 Now let's look at an annotated diagram of the water cycle. This is an example of writing to explain a process.

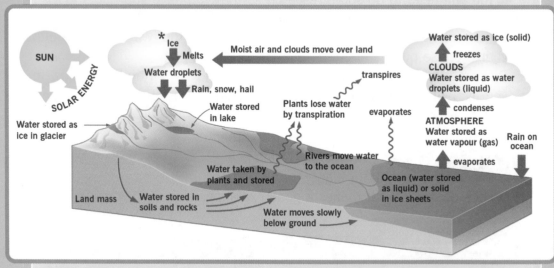

2 With a partner, study the diagram.
- Is there a correct order for the water cycle process? Does it matter where you start in the process?
- Why is this important in the explanation?
- How does one point lead on to another?
- Look at the features of the writing and compare them to the list of features in the Introduction – impersonal, passive and so on.
- Is anything unclear? How could you improve it?

3 Working on you own, use the diagram to rewrite the information to provide an explanation of the water cycle process in a written, as opposed to a diagrammatic, form. You can of course still use illustrations or your own diagrams, but you must use words to explain the process.

- You should give the information in the form of short paragraphs.
- Your audience will be students in Year 6, so consider what words and processes they will understand.
- Use some of the techniques listed above in the Introduction – think about the key issues and the order in which they will appear.
- Difficult technical words will need explanation from a dictionary.

4 Try explaining one of these:

- The life cycle of a frog – from egg to tadpole to frog
- How a volcano is formed
- The principle of a car engine
- How an aeroplane flies
- How the first men got to the moon in 1969.

It might be helpful to talk about your possible choice with a friend. Can you anticipate any problems you might have?

- You will need to do some research so that you have your facts to report and explain. Where will you do your research?
- Try to find an annotated diagram to enhance your explanation.
- Plan very carefully what you are going to say. Plan some numbered headings and try to ensure that you cover one point per paragraph.
- Look again at the technical points in the Introduction. Build some of these techniques into your final draft. Think especially about connectives. They will make your argument flow.
- Include a diagram, drawn or scanned.
- Check your writing for clarity, order and accuracy.

Review

- Sum up what have you learned about writing to explain?
- Think about your school textbooks for various subjects. Which textbooks use explanatory writing most often and which do you find most useful?

Describing people and places

Aims

- To look at descriptive writing.
- To study descriptive techniques so that we know how to describe an object, person or setting in a way that includes relevant details and is accurate and evocative.

Starter session

Think of a place that you really like. It might be a glamorous holiday destination, or something quite ordinary: the bottom of your garden or a corner of the park.

On a piece of paper, write down the name or brief description about your chosen place, and three things you like about it.

Your teacher will ask six volunteers to read out what they have written.

Introduction

'Evoke' and 'evocative' are good words to use when you are describing a remembered place.

> *'Evoke'* is a verb, meaning 'recall to mind'.

> *'Evocative'* is an adjective meaning 'recalling to mind scenes, memories and feelings'.

When you remember your favourite place, you evoke it.

How can you write an evocative description of it?

Good description depends on good observation.

Nature has given us *five senses* to observe the world:

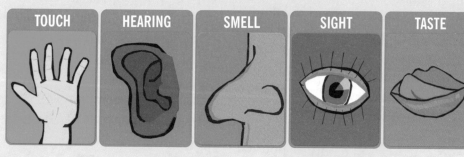

| TOUCH | HEARING | SMELL | SIGHT | TASTE |

- Discuss with a partner how you would rank these in order of importance?

Well-chosen details observed through the five senses are going to make your description vivid.

Remember:
- **Similes** are direct comparisons, starting with 'like' or 'as'.
- **Metaphors** are suggested or implied comparisons.

INFORMATION

- **Adjectives** (that describe nouns) and **adverbs** (that describe verbs) are obviously vital in description.
- **Colours** are particularly important.
- **Verbs** (doing or being words) are another key element.
- **Comparisons** will help the reader to picture your place.

Development

1 Read this descriptive passage from **'Hound of the Baskervilles'** (Text 1) by Sir Arthur Conan Doyle, creator of the detective, Sherlock Holmes. This is our first glimpse of Baskerville Hall on Dartmoor where a frightening, ghostly Hound has terrified the owner to death.

TEXT 1

HOUND OF THE BASKERVILLES (extract)

There rose ever, dark against the evening sky, the long, gloomy curve of the moor, broken by the jagged and sinister hills […] To me a tinge of melancholy lay upon the countryside, which bore so clearly the mark of the waning year. Yellow leaves carpeted the lanes and fluttered down upon us as we passed. The rattle of our wheels died away as we drove through drifts of rotting vegetation […] Our wagonette had topped a rise and in front of us rose the huge expanse of the moor, mottled with gnarled and craggy cairns and tors. A cold wind swept down from it and set us shivering […] Two high, narrow towers rose over the trees. The driver pointed with his whip. 'Baskerville Hall,' said he […]

Through the gateway we passed into the avenue, where the wheels were again hushed amid the leaves, and the old trees shot their branches in a sombre tunnel over our heads. Baskerville shuddered as he looked up the long, dark drive to where the house glimmered like a ghost at the farther end […]

2 Which three of the five senses help to make this passage so strongly descriptive? Find exact examples of:

- Colours
- A simile and some metaphors
- Ten adjectives that you admire
- Three verbs that help create the sinister mood.

3 Now turn back to your own chosen place – the place you thought and wrote about in the Starter session.

4 On paper, write down:

- Ten details that you remember *seeing* there
- Six things you *heard* in this place
- Six points from your memories of the *taste*, *smell and touch* of the location (this is not just hands: it can be the shock of cold sea on your body, or the feel of pebbles underfoot).

5 Your teacher will ask six volunteers to read their lists aloud to the class.

- Did you like the details?
- Could you picture the place the reader was describing?
- How would you have improved it?

6 Now let's think about colours:

- When you are thinking about your special place, do any comparisons come to mind (such as 'The sea was as green as...') ?
- Remember that a good comparison is accurate, appropriate and yet fresh.
- Adjective, adverb and verb research needs to be done with a thesaurus. Ask your teacher how to use one if you are unsure.

7 Now you have enough notes to write an evocative description of your chosen place. Your teacher may ask you to do this for homework.

- Your description should be one side of A4 paper at most.
- Keep to description and avoid story-telling!
- Past tense fits with memory well but present tense can be dramatic.

8 When you have finished your draft description, check it thoroughly.

- Have you put in enough details to make the place really come alive?

Review

Remind yourself of the key points of descriptive writing.
- Think about which element is the most important to you.
- Put your hand up and say why.
- Are your views different to those of your classmates?

Finally, think of places or settings in books that you have read.
- Choose one you remember well.
- Your teacher will ask volunteers to tell the class about this setting and why it is memorable.
- Are the examples similar or different? Why?

Advertising

Aims

- To study advertisements that use persuasive writing.
- To look at their persuasive techniques such as reiteration, exaggeration, repetition and the use of rhetorical questions.

Starter session

In your last lesson your teacher will have given you the task of finding, and bringing to school, three eye-catching advertisements in a newspaper or magazine. They should include quite a lot of wording, a picture and a bold heading. We are going to look at your clippings now.

Working in groups of four, you should take it in turns to choose one advertisement and tell your friends what it is about and what is interesting about it. Do your classmates agree with you?

Introduction

When modern advertising was invented, at the end of the nineteenth and beginning of the twentieth centuries, businesses wanted to place adverts everywhere:

- By writing on the White Cliffs of Dover
- By putting up posters in the countryside
- By drawing slogans in smoke from aeroplanes in the sky.

Luckily, these were not allowed, but advertising still surrounds us today. In groups of four, consider where you see advertisements in your everyday surroundings.

1 Make a list together.
2 Compare your lists across the class.
3 Discuss which method of advertising has most effect on you.

Development

Now study this advertisement for home cinema.

the ultimate experience in
Home Cinema Entertainment
technology

see it! hear it! feel it!

VISIT OUR NEW DEDICATED HOME CINEMA SHOWROOM

- LARGE RANGE OF PLASMA SCREENS from 32" — 50"
- LCD SCREENS from 15" — 30"
- HIGH QUALITY RANGE OF HOME CINEMA SYSTEMS — AV AMPS — SPEAKERS — LIFESTYLE HOME THEATRE MODULES

SONY
UK
Dealer of the Year
2001

EP

109 BROADWAY
BEXLEYHEATH
(Broadway Shopping Centre)

020 8298 7880

OPEN 7 DAYS
Thurs till 8.00pm

Our experienced staff can advise on a huge range of products and provide the ideal solution to your requirements

1 In your group of four, identify the persuasive methods (of language, layout or picture) used to influence the reader. Look again at the Introduction if you need to remind yourself of the techniques advertisers use.

---

2 Now let's think about creating your own advertisement. Choose one of these ideas:

- You want to sell a new micro city-car. It has room for two, is economical to run and parks very easily. It is for shopping, visits and business journeys. Usually people do not like such vehicles. How are you going to overcome their reluctance with persuasive language, layout and illustrations.
- You want tourists to come to a British holiday destination, in town, country or seaside. You have a problem: most people want to go abroad to seek out the sun. Make your points appealing and eye-catching.
- Imagine you are the manager of a new pop group. It is about to launch its first single. Design an advertisement that will tempt young people into buying this record. Remember to think of a catchy name for the group, and a slogan!

3 Now let's start thinking about the advert.

- On your own, prepare rough notes by jotting down about six main ideas as a star chart.
- Then redraft the numbered points in order.
- Now think about a heading, slogan and picture.
- How are you going to use rhetorical devices? Check the list in the Introduction.
- Find places for some or all of these in your plan.

4 Now write a first full draft. Paragraphs should be short and sentences crisp.

5 With a partner, read your drafts together. What should you add or leave out?

6 Alter your notes in the light of your partner's comments.

7 Compose the final draft of your advertisement. Your teacher may ask you to do this for homework. Remember to check the detail and presentation when you finish.

Review

You have looked at the many ways in which persuasive writing tries to influence us. Look again at the three advertisements you brought to school. Can you now see more in them? Which one now seems the best?

Finally, think about television commercials. Can you think of one that made a big impression on you? Put up your hand and tell the class about it.

Using evidence

Aims

- To study written arguments.
- To look at the methods and techniques of argument such as using statistical evidence, exemplification and testimony.
- To go on to write an argument using these methods.

Starter session

- What is a **'controversy'**?
- Put up your hand and suggest an answer to the rest of the class. Your teacher will brainstorm ideas and make a list of key features on the board.
- With a partner, write a list of controversial subjects that have been in the news lately. Which one are you most interested in? Underline this. You could argue for or against this. Which side will you be on?

Introduction

In debates you argue about controversial subjects.

To win an argument, you would need stronger points than the other side and you would use more skill in the way you present those points. Argument is therefore a form of persuasion (if you are unsure about this term have another look at Unit 8). In this case you are persuading people to accept your point of view.

INFORMATION

A written argument uses the same techniques as persuasion. It, too, employs rhetorical devices (tricks of persuasive language):

- **Repetition** of key words, phrases and ideas
- **Rhetorical questions** that expect a certain answer
- Use of **vivid examples** (exemplification):
  'If you had seen the terrible accident that I saw on the M11, you would hate motor vehicles as I do....'
- Use of facts and figures (**statistical** evidence)
- A build up of a series of points to a **climax**:
  'The mobile phone is a nuisance, a cause of crime, a health hazard, and, above all, a killer when used by drivers on the road...'
- **Personal details** to set against general points (testimony):
  'I myself saw the horrible effects of smoking when my grandad died...'

Writing to support an argument has its own **style**:

- A good argument makes **clear points**, supported by **evidence**, in **ordered paragraphs**.
- **Connectives** (linking words and phrases) between paragraphs are important, especially if the argument is to be read out.
- Arguments need to start with a brief **introduction** saying which side you are on.
- A good **conclusion** reminds the reader and/or listener of your main points, and it would appeal for audience support.
- If it is a live debate, you will have to add **last minute answers** to opposition points.

Development

1 Look at these **controversial topics** with a partner:

- Should school uniform be abolished?
- Is the motor vehicle a curse or a blessing?
- Are mobile phones a good idea or a menace?
- Does television do more harm than good?

- Which are you going to choose?
- Which side are you going to be on?

2 Having chosen, work alone to make a plan of six points for a debate, speech or article for the school magazine.

- Remember to keep to one side or the other!
- Try to make your points challenging.

Here are a few suggestions:

Uniform gives you pride
in your school
or
It embarrasses
poor families

Motor vehicles kill people
in great numbers
or
Ambulances and fire
engines save life

Mobile phones keep you in
touch with friends and family
or
They are a major cause
of juvenile crime

Television brings us the World
Cup and the Olympics live
or
It damages our eyes and
makes us 'couch potatoes'

3 Now do some library research and find some evidence to support these general ideas.

4 You could also interview classmates to gain some personal testimony, or design a simple questionnaire to work out some statistics.

5 Check over the technical points made in the Introduction above.
- Where can you put your questions and repetitions?
- Which connectives will you use to tie your paragraphs together?

6 When you have mapped out your six paragraphs, think about the introduction and conclusion. A summing up, that reminds us of your ideas, is always useful.

7 When you finish the final draft, test your article or speech by reading it aloud:
- Does it flow?
- Have you tried to use features of the persuasive style?

> **Bear in mind the following:**
> - Your article or speech need not be long.
> - People cannot concentrate for too long! One or two sides of A4 paper would be enough.
> - If it is a speech then the tone can be fairly colloquial (chatty), but the main points need to be forceful and memorable.

Review

End with an argument 'quickie'!

In the Starter session, you might have mentioned these controversies:
- Fox hunting
- Euthanasia (mercy killing)
- Charging motorists to enter cities
- Top footballers' huge salaries.

Put up your hand and say three things for or against one of these topics. Someone respond with three points. Then do another...

That's good advice

Aims

- To study writing intended to advise us.
- To look at the techniques and qualities of this style of writing such as anticipating the needs, interests and views of the intended reader.

Starter session

Spend a minute on your own, thinking about the differences between the three words below.

'advise' is the verb; 'advice' is the noun

- Advise • Persuade • Instruct

Your teacher will then ask you to volunteer your ideas to the class and will make a list of the key points of each word. Then as a class, you can discuss the differences. When everyone is happy with the definitions, write them in your exercise book.

Introduction

1 With a partner, discuss who gives us advice in our own lives. Make a list of these sources of advice.

- Don't forget magazine articles, government advertisements on TV, official leaflets that you find at the dentist's or doctor's, at the vet's, or in the library.

2 Look back at your three definitions of persuade, instruct and advise. As you probably worked out, in advice suggestions are made and information given. The person advised can accept or disregard these. If the dentist **advises** you to clean your teeth, you do not have to do so!

INFORMATION

Now let's think about the **qualities of good advice writing**:

- It has a strong **sense of audience**, of the people it's aimed at.
- Its **style and tone** are suitable for that audience.
- It makes **key points**, perhaps shown as headings.
- Each of these is backed up with **evidence**.
- The heading and its evidence make up the **paragraph**.
- You want to put your points across **clearly**:
  i   Use **plain** words
  ii **Short** sentences will have impact
  iii **Presentation** is important to make people read your advice.

Development

Now we are going to start to think about making our own piece of writing to advise.

School transfer is a good subject.

- You remember how difficult and worrying it seemed to be to move from primary to secondary school?
- You probably received all kinds of good advice.
- Perhaps the most valuable came from young people who had just passed through the transfer themselves.

Your task is to write a letter to a Year 6 pupil, giving her or him advice about the move from primary to secondary school.

1 In groups of four, discuss the difficulties and anxieties, real and imagined, of the move from primary to secondary school.

2 Make a long list of these anxieties. Include such things as:
   - New friendships
   - Lots of new subjects
   - A different teacher for each subject
   - More homework
   - New uniform
   - Choosing and using the right equipment … and so on.

3 Now reconsider the list. Which **six items** would you personally see as most important? Underline these on your list. These will make the six paragraph themes for your letter.

4 Now, working on your own, make a plan for your letter.
   - Each paragraph begins with a statement and follows it up with supporting evidence.

   For example:

Bullying is not a problem at our school.
We have an anti-bullying policy that we've copied into our school planners. The Head often talks about it in assembly. Teachers follow up any complaint. Anyone who tries to bully is dealt with severely. So there's no need to worry about bullies!

- When you compose each paragraph, think about **style**.
- Keep the **sentences short** and use **plain words**.
- **Colloquialisms** (words and phrases from chatty, everyday speech) would be acceptable here. You can use short forms (won't, don't, didn't, we've etc).
- Be **positive** and friendly, like the secondary school itself.
- You need some sort of **introduction**:

Your class/group

School address

Date

Dear_____,

I'm really glad to hear that you're coming up to our school next September. It's a big change in your life. I'm sending some advice and information to help you enjoy the move and to calm any fears you might have......

- Then your six paragraphs follow.
- Sign off in a cheerful way at the end and promise to look out for her or him after the summer holidays.

5 Now you need to write your final draft – perhaps for homework.

- If you do it in ICT, think hard about presentational devices.
- Check the detail very carefully – it would not be impressive to send a Year 6 pupil a letter full of mistakes!
- Remember: if you actually send or e-mail this letter, do get your teacher to look it over first. Your idea of a joke could easily be a Year 6 pupil's nightmare!

Review

- Remind yourself of the differences between 'advise', 'persuade' and 'instruct'.
- Where, in school, would you be instructed and where advised?
- Make your points to the rest of the class.
- What advice do you ignore and what do you follow? What **really** useful advice have you received? Tell the class.

UNIT 11

Applying to join the school council

Aims

- To consider the nature of writing to analyse (that is, evaluating a particular situation, object or event and presenting findings fairly and giving a personal view).
- To see how this form of writing works.

Starter session

'Analyse' is a difficult word.

- It means to look at something in detail, to understand it better.
- The dictionary says: *'To examine methodically and in detail the contents or structure of something'*.

Let us look at some people who analyse things:

- What would a football commentator look at to analyse how Arsenal, for example, plays in a game of football?
- What would a drama critic look at to analyse the performance of a play?
- What would a detective look at to analyse the evidence against a murder suspect?

Choose one of these people and volunteer your comments to the class.

Try to bring in the idea of 'detail'. Your teacher will write down your suggestions on the board.

Introduction

Analysing a text involves looking at the information (be it a performance or a piece of writing) **methodically** and **in detail**.

> *methodically*: you go step by step in an orderly way

> *in detail*: you use even small points as evidence to back up your argument

If you are comparing written statements, then you need a set of **'criteria'**: principles or standards used to judge something.

> Note: the singular of 'criteria' is 'criterion'

Imagine that there is an election to choose a Year 7 member of the school council at Sunnyhill Community College. A pupil who wishes to be considered has to write an application letter, saying why she or he should be chosen.

Later on, you and a partner are going to read these letters and choose the best candidate for the School Council.
- First discuss together what **criteria** you are going to use to judge the applicants.
- What qualities would you expect a member of the council to have (reliability, realistic ideas, ability to express her or himself, and so on)?
- You need six to eight points.

Development

1 Now read the application letters below:

CHARLOTTE

My name is Charlotte Smith. I would like to put myself forward for the council. I am very hard-working and enjoy maths, science and English particularly. I spend a lot of time on homework and have gained the highest number of merit awards in my Year Group. I recently got Grade 5 piano. I go to Guides every week. I also shop for an elderly neighbour. I have a few close friends who share my interests. I think everyone should work hard and behave sensibly.

KEVIN

My name is Kevin and I'd really like to be on the council. I try quite hard in lessons and almost always do my homework, although sometimes it's late in. I love football and play every lunch-time with my mates (boys only). I would ask for lots of new things like finishing at two o'clock, with Wednesday afternoons off so that we can play footy or go fishing.

TINA

I'm Tina and my mates all reckon I'd be dead good at being on the council because I can always make myself heard. I've got loads of opinions about loads of things and I don't care who hears them. I'm really popular and I've got loads of mates. I'm really confident and would find it easy to get the council to do what I want them to do. If you want to ban uniform, homework and detentions, then vote for me – a voice that will be heard.

MILADUR

My name is Miladur and I would like as many people as possible to vote for me to be on the council. During my time at Sunnyhill Community College, I have always shown that I am reliable and that I work hard. I am in the football team and play in the College band. Outside school, I play for the local Under 16s football team.

I enjoy school a lot, and have many friends. I am easy to get on with and work well with others. I have many ideas for improving life at the College and I would enjoy working closely with other students and teachers to make things better. I would like, for example, to see a wider choice in the canteen. I have ideas for school trips and better social facilities for breaks and lunchtimes.

Vote Miladur for a sunnier Sunnyhill!

2 Now, still working with your partner, analyse the letters, using your criteria.

● If your first criterion is reliability, then look for evidence of that in each letter. For example, write down the words or sentences from the letter that show that reliability.

- Do the same for your other criteria. You could do this in a chart form with your criteria in columns and the candidates in rows. You could give each candidate a score for each criterion and write down in the chart the key words and phrases to support your argument. For example:

candidate	reliability	realistic ideas	good expression
Charlotte			
Kevin			
Tina			
Miladur			

- It should be possible after this analysis of the detail of the letter to say which candidate is the best.

3 Now we're going to think about a piece of analysis writing – your teacher may give you this exercise for homework.
You are going to prepare a report for the Headteacher explaining your choice of candidates for the school council.

You will need to follow something like this structure:
- A brief **introduction** explaining your criteria
- **Four paragraphs** (one for each candidate)
- A short **conclusion**, summing up your choice
- You could quote details from the letters to support your choice.

Review

You have learned that **writing to analyse** involves going over the evidence in methodical **order** including **details** from the text to support your conclusions.

- In which school subjects would you use writing to analyse? Discuss this as a class.
- Try to think of particular examples of such writing.

Film review

Aims

● To study the style, methods and techniques of writing used to review a written or media text.

Starter session

Some texts are in printed form: novel, newspaper story, magazine article, short story, poem, printed play, comic strip and so on.

Others come to us through the media: film, television, video, DVD, Internet, radio programme, audio tape.

With a partner, fill in examples in this list of media texts:

Text type	Title	Intended audience
pre-twentieth-century novel		
poem		
TV soap opera		
film		
football sports report		
cartoon story		
TV documentary		
twentieth/twenty-first-century novel		

Introduction

A review needs a clear structure if it is to tell the audience what it wants to know. If you were reviewing a novel, short story or play, you would need these ideas:

● The **facts** about the book (title, date, author)
● A very **brief outline** of the story

- Details about the main **characters**: what they are like
- Information about the **setting**: time and place
- What is **good** about the text?
- What are its **weaknesses**?
- Who is the intended **audience**?
- What is the final **verdict**?

A **film review** would include many of these ideas, too.

Read Text 1, Barry Norman's review of the film *Time Machine*.

TEXT 1

TIME MACHINE

In effect there are two films here. The first takes place in early-20th-century New York, the second in the same – though now totally unrecognisable – place 800,000 years hence. Well, as H.G. Wells, the writer of the original story taught us, you can do that with a time machine.

In the first part, something nasty happens to Sienna Guillory, the fiancee of absent minded professor Guy Pearce, so he builds his machine to nip back in time to see if he can change things. He can't.

Undaunted, he whizzes off into the future to find out why he can't alter the past. But, my word, things are different. What was once New York is now a sort of jungle where the nice brown-skinned Eloi, personified by Samantha Mumba, live above ground and the vicious, semi-human Morlocks lurk under it and use the Eloi for food. A chalk-white Jeremy Irons is the leader of this gang.

Director Simon Wells, great-grandson of H. G., employs spectacular effects and nifty time-lapse photography – especially in the first half, which is much the more interesting. The second half has Pearce becoming a sort of Indiana Jones and offers conventional action-packed, summer blockbuster fare.

It's all pretty good fun, though.

This review has a clear, well-ordered structure.

1 What does the reviewer say on the points we looked at above? Put up your hand to answer.

- Who made the film?
- Where is it set in place and time?
- What technical effects are used to make the film impressive?
- Who stars in the film?
- It is a film with two halves. Which is better? Why is this?
- What is Barry Norman's final verdict on the film?
- How would you describe the written style of this review?

If you were writing about a **printed text**, you might include something about length of sentences and paragraphs, vocabulary, etc. Film also has its **technical language**. Knowing some of these terms may help you say how the film works and why it affects you strongly:

Shot: a single picture taken by the camera
Sequence: a series of shots
Cut: the movement from one shot to another
Pan: the camera moves across a scene or landscape
Close-up: the camera moves in close to a face, or detail of the scene
Soundtrack: the voices, noises and music

Of these, the **sequence** is the most important: sudden cuts from a girl ti to a track to an approaching train, fo example, make the heart beat faster you watch.

Development

You are going to write a **review of a film** you have seen recently at the cinema or on television. You'll need to prepare carefully.

1 Discuss with a partner films that you have seen that might be suitable for your review.
   - Try to avoid the obvious, but do choose a film you know well or one that you could, perhaps, watch again on video at home.

2 Then, working on your own, make a plan of your main points.
   - You could use some of ideas from the Introduction.
   - Make sure you know what audience you are aiming at.
   - Look closely at the opening.

Here are some possible ideas for the first paragraph:

_____ was directed by_____. It is
about_____ (very brief outline: do not give away any twists or
surprise ending). It stars_____...

3 Now let's think about the other paragraphs – you'll need to make about six further points.
   - Include something about striking **shots** or **sequences**.
   - What was interesting about the **soundtrack** and **music**?

4 When you have your outline notes, discuss them with a partner.
   - Are there any things you feel you should add or take away?
   - Do not make your review too long: about one side of A4 paper will be enough.

5 Now you're going to write the final version of your review. (You might need to do a little more research on your film before you start.)
   - Read over your final version, checking it carefully.
   - Make sure it is lively and suitable for your intended audience.

Review

- Think about the differences between written and film texts.
- Can you suggest some popular books that have become films?
- Compare the film and text versions and volunteer your comparison comments to the class. If you can include any technical film words, do so!

Narration

Aims

- To look again at writing to narrate.
- To examine the role of the narrator.
- To write part of a story told by two narrators.

Starter session

Read the following descriptions of two characters:

Jane is 36. She is Emma's mother. Emma wants to go to a party at a local club to celebrate a friend's eighteenth birthday. Jane does not want her to go. It is a Wednesday night and Emma has to go to school the following day. Most of the people who will be at the party are older than Emma and some of them have bad reputations. The club was recently raided by the police.

Emma, 15, is Jane's daughter. She knows that some of the people who are going to the party have been in trouble and that the club has attracted the attention of the police. She also knows that she is far too sensible to be drawn into any bad behaviour by others. Even though the party is on a Wednesday night and will not end until late, she thinks that she will have no problems about getting up for school on Thursday.

- In pairs, improvise the scene where Emma asks Jane if she can go to the party.
- Working alone, write the two first–person accounts of the conversation, one as if you are Emma and one as if you are Jane. Here are some sentence starters which might help you:

Jane
- I couldn't believe what she was asking me...
- Why does she have to hang around with people like that?
- I've always done my best for her...
- My little girl....
- I don't know what her father will say...

Emma

- Honestly, it's not as if I'm a baby....
- Doesn't she trust me?
- She should be glad I told her! I could have just gone!
- Those were my friends she was talking about! She made them sound as if...
- So, what club hasn't been raided by the police these days?

- In pairs, discuss the differences between Emma's and Jane's accounts of the conversation. What differences are there in their opinions about:
  – The club
  – The friends
  – The importance of Emma's age
  – Whether Emma should go to the party or not.

Introduction

Novels use various forms of narration.

- **The authorial voice**: the author observes his characters from the outside, sometimes allowing you to share their thoughts.
  Example: *Lord of the Flies* by William Golding
- The narrator is **one of the characters**: we see events through his or her eyes. Example: Pip in *Great Expectations* by Charles Dickens
- **Several characters** tell the story, with their different viewpoints.
  Example: *The Woman in White* by Wilkie Collins

Development

Robert Swindells, the contemporary novelist, uses **two narrators** to tell the story of this novel, *Stone Cold* (Text 1). One is Link, a homeless teenage boy who lives on the streets of London. The other is a far more sinister character called Shelter.

Here are two extracts from the novel, the first narrated by Link and the second by Shelter:

STONE COLD (extract)

Link

After a bit I came to a doorway which was both deep and unoccupied. I dodged into it and stood there, wondering whether I dare doss down. What if this was somebody's bedroom too? Somebody big, like the scouser? Suppose he showed up and took a fancy to my pack, my bed-roll, and demanded them? Or he might just knife me and take them. On the other hand it was now pretty late, though of course I didn't know what time exactly. Surely, I told myself, if somebody dossed down here regularly he'd be here by now? Any way, I was dead tired. I had to get my head down somewhere, and wherever I went there was going to be this same doubt. So.

I'd just wriggled into my sleeping-bag and dropped my head on my pack when he arrived. I heard these footsteps and thought, keep going. Go past. Please go past, but he didn't. The footsteps stopped and I knew he was looking down at me. I opened my eyes. He was just a shadow framed in the doorway. 'This your place?' I croaked. Stupid question. He was going to say yes even if it wasn't, right?...I wondered how big he was.

'No, you're right, mate.' He sounded laid back, amiable. 'Just shove up a bit so I can spread my roll.' I obliged and he settled himself beside me, so close we were almost touching. It felt good to be with someone. Now, if anybody else turned up it wouldn't matter. There were two of us...

Shelter

I've been out tonight. I took the tube down to Charing Cross and walked about a bit. Tour of inspection, you might say.

And I found them, as I'd known I would. Hundreds of the scruffy blighters, lying around making the place look manky. I marched along the Strand and there they were, dossing in all the doorways – even Lloyds Bank and the Law Courts.

One cheeky little bugger – couldn't have been more than seventeen – actually asked me for money. Have you got any change, he says. I looked him up and down and I said, 'Change? I'd change you, my lad, if I had you in khaki for six weeks.' It didn't go in, though. He just smiled and said have a nice night...

National Service. That was the thing. It brought 'em all in – the teds, the rockers, the Mammy's boys. And it changed 'em, by golly it did. In six weeks. There were no teddy boys on that passing-out parade I can tell you, and no rockers, either. Soldiers, that's what it made of 'em. There were no exceptions.

And that was my mission in life – to turn dirty, scruffy, pimply youths into soldiers. Into men. And I did it, too. Year after year.

1 In pairs, find as many clues as you can about the two characters' feelings, attitudes and personalities.

2 Now, working alone, think about a story with two narrators. You are going to write a passage as seen through the eyes of two contrasting people.

- Each narrator will be 'I'.
- You must suggest their differences through their thoughts, observations and opinions.

Here are some possible situations:

- A criminal on the run on a remote moorland, and the detective who is relentlessly hunting him.
- A boy and a girl who have very different ideas about their relationship.
- A young bride's view of her wedding contrasted with that of her father.
- A famous star's thoughts on a concert, and those of an obsessive fan.
- A ten-year-old child's view of a French holiday beach in Normandy, and her/his grandfather's thoughts about that same beach where he fought on D-Day in June 1944.

Each passage may be one or two paragraphs. If you are going to use speech, set it out correctly:

- Put inverted commas around the actual words spoken
- Each new speaker starts a new paragraph.

3 After preparing rough notes, complete the final draft for homework.

Review

There are many elements in a good narrative:

- An arresting opening
- A good story-line
- Character
- Setting
- Narrative viewpoint
- Strong conclusion.

Which of these do you think is most important to hold the interest of the reader? Try to think of examples from books that you have read. Discuss this as a class.

Figurative language

Aims

- To learn how to use figurative language, such as metaphors and similes, when describing places and characters.

Starter session

It is a hot summer day. You and your friends are out walking when you come across some cool, shady woods. There is a stream, birds singing and the scent of flowers.

- Brainstorm words on the board to describe what you can see, hear, feel and smell. Here are some words to start you off:
  - Trees – rustling, gentle, green, casting dappled shade, full of life.
  - Stream – flowing, bubbling
  - Birds – chirping, singing

Now divide your words into two groups: literal and figurative.

INFORMATION

- **Literal language** uses only the basic meaning of a word without any comparison involved, e.g. 'I could see the stars in the night sky'.
- **Figurative language** uses special effects of writing, such as similes, metaphors and personification.
- A **simile** is a direct comparison. It usually starts with 'like' or 'as', e.g. 'The stars looked like sand thrown at velvet'.
- A **metaphor** is an implied or suggested comparison. There is no 'like' or 'as', e.g. 'The sky was peppered with stars'.
- **Personification** describes an idea of thing by giving it human qualities, e.g. 'A crowd of stars stared solemnly'.

Literal	Figurative

Introduction

The same place can be made to seem welcoming, threatening, mysterious or romantic, depending on how you, as a writer, want your readers to see it.

Use this writing frame to write two different descriptions of a house. The first should make it seem welcoming and pleasant, the second should make it seem threatening and sinister.

The old house sat in the middle of the garden like _____. Its windows were _____. As I walked up to the front door I noticed _____. The door opened with a noise like _____ and I went into the _____ interior. The walls were hung with _____ and I noticed _____ on the floor. The air smelt faintly of _____ and I became aware of the noise of _____. Glancing in the old mirror above the fireplace I noticed a figure. I whirled round to face it and to my surprise I found myself face to face with _____.

Development

1 Divide into pairs. One of you will work on Text 1 and the other on Text 2. Text 1 is from the opening of the play *Under Milk Wood* by Dylan Thomas and describes the Welsh village where the play is set.

TEXT 1

UNDER MILK WOOD (extract)

It is spring, moonless night in the small town, starless and bible-black, the cobblestreets silent and the hunched, courters'-and-rabbits' wood limping invisible down to the sloeblack, slow, black, crowblack, fishingboat-bobbing sea. The houses are blind as moles (though moles see fine to-night in the snouting, velvet dingles) or blind as Captain Cat there in the muffled middle by the pump and the town clock, the shops in mourning, the Welfare Hall in widow's weeds. And all the people of the lulled and dumbfound town are sleeping now.
[...] And the anthracite statues of the horses sleep in the fields, and the cows in the byres, and the dogs in the wetnosed yards; and the cats nap in the slant corners or lope sly, streaking and needling, on the one cloud of the roofs.

In Text 2, Sylvia Plath is describing her child using only figurative language. She describes the child's character rather than appearance.

TEXT 2

YOU'RE

Clownlike, happiest on your hands,
Feet to the stars, and moon-skulled,
Gilled like a fish. A common-sense
Thumbs-down on the dodo's mode.
Wrapped up in yourself like a spool,
Trawling your dark as owls do.
Mute as a turnip from the Fourth
Of July to All Fool's Day,
O high-riser, my little loaf.

Vague as fog and looked for like mail.
Farther off than Australia.
Bent-backed Atlas, our travelled prawn.
Snug as a bud and at home
Like a sprat in a pickle jug.
A creel of eels, all ripples.
Jumpy as a Mexican bean.
Right, like a well-done sum.
A clean slate, with your own face on.

2 In pairs, copy and complete this grid for either extract.

	3 examples	Effect created by each example
Metaphors		
Similes		
Personification		

3 With your partner, discuss both extracts. Concentrate on:

- The interesting words, especially adjectives and verbs
- The figurative language, especially comparisons.

Review

- In your pairs, read and discuss your descriptions of the house created in the Introduction.
- Can you suggest any improvements?
- Bearing these suggestions in mind, write a final draft of your description.

Traditional tales

Aims

- To examine the 'rules' for writing fairy stories.
- To use your imagination to update one of these stories by breaking the rules.
- To experiment with language in order to create a specific tone in your writing.

Starter session

Here are some plot conventions and common phrases found in fairy tales.

- As a class, add as many items as you can to the list:
    - There is always a happy ending
    - Once upon a time...
    - All stepmothers are wicked
    - Beautiful princess.

> A **convention** in literature is a widely used and accepted way of writing something.

- In pairs, brainstorm as many fairy tales as you can. Do they fit these conventions?

Introduction

Read the following version of the story of *Goldilocks and the Three Bears*.

TEXT **1**

GOLDILOCKS AND THE THREE BEARS

Yesterday I went out for a walk with my wife and son – as per usual – and you won't believe what happened.

When we got back we walked into the kitchen and got a terrible shock. It was a complete tip. Some little vandal calling herself 'Goldilox' (she'd sprayed it all over the walls) had totally ransacked the place.

We'd left our dinner out on the table so we could eat it when we got back. The greedy cow had microwaved each meal and taken huge munches out of each one.

Well obviously I said, 'Who's been eating my Big Mac?' and my wife said, 'Who's been eating my Middle Mac?' and the baby wanted to know who'd been munching his Kid's Club burger.

The bathroom was just shocking – water all over the floor. And I couldn't help roaring, 'Who's been splashing in my jaccuzzi?', and my wife said the same, and so did my son.

We walked in a daze through the entire house – we were all in shock, as you can imagine. And when we got to the bedroom...there she was in the baby's bed! You could see her dark roots sticking out from under the duvet. The nerve of her!

Well I roared at her and she woke up. But she was as slippery as an eel and made a get-away through the French window. We phoned the police, but there's very little they can do about teenage vandals.

In pairs identify, all the ways in which this story breaks the conventions of fairy tales.

Development

1 When modern ideas, language or objects are introduced into an old text they are called **anachronisms**. Read Text 2, which is the beginning of the famous tale **Rumpelstiltskin**.

> An *anachronism* means placing something in a time in history to which it does not belong: for example, an aeroplane in Roman times.

TEXT 2

RUMPELSTILTSKIN (extract)

<u>There was once a miller</u> who was very poor, but he had <u>a beautiful daughter</u>. <u>Now it fell out</u> that he chanced to speak with <u>the King</u>, and in order to give himself an air of importance he said: 'I have a daughter who <u>can spin gold out of straw</u>.'

The king said to the miller: 'That's an art in which I'm much interested. If your daughter's as skilful as you say she is, bring her to my <u>castle</u> tomorrow and I'll put her to the test.'

Accordingly, when the girl was brought to the castle, The King conducted her to a chamber which was quite full of straw, gave her a <u>spinning-wheel and winder</u>, and said, 'Now, set to work, and if between tonight and tomorrow at dawn you have not spun this straw into gold you must die.' <u>Thereupon</u> he carefully locked the door of the <u>chamber</u> and she remained alone.

2 Rewrite the passage, replacing the underlined words and phrases with modern words, characters and skills.

51

3 We are now going to take a fairy story or traditional tale and re-write it, breaking as many rules as we can.

- Let's think about **gender** stereotypes. How about starting with:

> 'Cinderello was an ugly, spoilt boy who lived with his wicked father and his beautiful, good, kind stepmother.'

- You could set your story in a totally different time or place. For example:

> 'Little Red Riding Hood did not want to visit her boring grandmother. She wanted to carry on playing games on her computer, so the first time her mother called her, she pretended not to hear...'

- You could re-write the story from a totally different point of view.

> 'Why I ever agreed to marry him, I'll never know. Well, I suppose he had plenty of money but he also had that dreadful daughter! 'Snow White' she was called. I mean, plain old Sandra or Betty would have been good enough for most people, but imagine calling your child 'Snow White'! ...

4 Now, in pairs, discuss which fairy story you are going to update.

- What will you change – character, time, plot?
- How will you change it?

5 Prepare a draft of your story and present it to your partner.

- How could your story be improved?

6 Write up your final version of the updated fairy tale. Your teacher will ask some of you to read them to the class. Which ones do you like best and why?

Review

Fairy tales tend to follow a set of rules or conventions. In pairs, discuss what effect it has on a fairy tale when words and phrases, events, characters and objects that contradict these conventions are introduced.

YEAR **8** UNIT 4

Poetic forms

Aims

- To investigate different forms of poetry.
- To experiment with the use of different forms and styles of poetry.

Starter session

There are many different forms of poetical structure.
In pairs, list as many different poetical forms and styles as you can. You may need to list types of poems and your teacher will help you with their names.

Introduction

Here are two epitaphs and two haiku.

Epitaph on a Tyrant (W.H. Auden)
Perfection, of a kind, was what he was after,
And the poetry he invented was easy to understand;
He knew human folly like the back of his hand,
And was greatly interested in armies and fleets;
And when he laughed, respectable senators burst with laughter,
And when he cried the little children died in the streets.

Jaffa (A. Rothapel)
Sun sets behind proud
Minarets. Turrets glow and
port illuminates.

A Cross-Road Epitaph (Amy Levy)
When first the world grew dark to me
I call'd on God, yet came not he.
Whereon, as wearier grew my lot,
On Love I call'd, but Love came not.
When a worse evil did befall,
Death, on thee only did I call.

Raspberry field (A. Rothapel)
Brambled thorny field
belies secret ruby blush.
Ripe berries within.

1 Working in pairs, write a set of instructions for writing an epitaph or a haiku. Include some information on the purpose of each poem.

2 Share your ideas with the class. Agree on the conventions or rules for each form and note them down.

Development

1 Using '**Anne Frank Huis**' (Text 1) as inspiration write a two-line epitaph for Anne Frank.

2 Think about the atmosphere of the Anne Frank Huis. Write a haiku about the setting.

BACKGROUND

Anne Frank Huis is in Amsterdam. It is the house where Anne Frank and her family hid from the Nazis during the Second World War. The family was betrayed in 1944 and Anne died in a concentration camp.

Anne kept a diary of her family's life in hiding and, by a miracle, it survived and was found by her father after the war and published. It is one of the most moving personal accounts ever published and became an international sensation.

 TEXT **1**

ANNE FRANK HUIS

Even now, after twice her lifetime of grief
and anger in the very place, whoever comes
to climb these narrow stairs, discovers how
the bookcase slides aside, then walks through
shadow into sunlit rooms, can never help

but break her secrecy again. Just listening
is a kind of guilt: the Westerkirk repeats
itself outside,as if all time worked round
towards her fear, and made each stroke die
down on guarded streets. Imagine it –

three years of whispering and loneliness
and plotting day by day, the Allied line
in Europe with a yellow chalk. What hope
she had for ordinary love and interest
survives her here, diplayed above the bed

as pictures of her family; some actors;
fashions chosen by Princess Elizabeth.
And those who stoop to see them find
not only patience missing its reward,
but one enduring wish for chances

like my own: to leave as simply
as I do, and walk at ease
up dusty tree-lined avenues, or watch
a silent barge come clear of bridges
settling their reflections in the blue canal.

Andrew Motion

Review

As a class, look back at your list of poetical forms and styles. Which form would you use for each of the following scenarios? Why?

- Your feelings of happiness when you see spring flowers in a field
- A knight who travels around the country doing brave deeds
- A pet that has died
- Your feelings of anxiety about a forthcoming examination.

School prospectus

Aims

- To look again at writing to inform.
- To revise points of technique in presenting information.
- To write an informative school prospectus leaflet.

Starter session

Imagine you are a pupil who is about to move school. On paper, write down five things that you would want to know about it and the things that your parents would want to know. Now share these points with the class, discussing the differing priorities of parents and their children.

Introduction

Look back at the earlier unit on writing to give information on page 16.

Revise what some of the key words in information writing mean:

facts   connectives   chronology   priority   style

Use your definitions to help you in this unit.

Development

1 Imagine you are going to write a prospectus sheet for your own school. With a partner, brainstorm what you are going to include. What are the vital points? Here are some starters:

INFORMATION

- School address
- School aims
- The building and facilities
- The time pattern of the day
- The curriculum (subjects studied)
- Any specialism?
- Homework policy
- Examinations and OFSTED report
- Uniform: what it consisits of
- Rewards and penalties
- Pastoral and staff structure
- Sport

2 Which items are you going to include in your leaflet (you may not have room for them all). What illustrations will you include?

3 Now, working alone, make a plan of your information leaflet. Think about the needs of the audience:

Future pupils   Parents   Governors   Visitors   Local press

- Have you a school motto, or a key aim, or an impressive quotation from an OFSTED report that you could highlight?

4 Strip down your notes to fit one side of A4 paper.

5 Discuss your notes with a partner.

- You might need to add or remove points.
- Think about priority: what is the best order for your ideas?
- Discuss your plans for illustrations and/or highlighted ideas or quotations.

6 Think about your language and style. Informative writing needs order and clarity. Plain language and simple sentences are going to help you cope with your varied audience.

7 Working alone, take your note structure and turn it into short paragraphs. Each should have a headline statement and other sentences giving more ideas and evidence about it. If the evidence goes best in a list, then use bullet points.

8 Now write a first draft of your leaflet.

9 Finally, think about presentation. Where will you put your eye-catching heading? Where will you place your illustrations?

10 Prepare your leaflet. Proofreading will be vital. A single spelling error will give a poor impression of the school.

Review

As a class, discuss what differences you would need in your prospectus sheet to make it suitable just for Year 6 pupils, rather than their parents.

A history of English

Aims

- To look again at writing to explain.
- To consider techniques to make writing easier to understand.
- To write an explanatory article for a specific audience.

Starter session

Read this strange rhyme (Text 1):

In pairs, using a dictionary, try to decipher what the rhyme means. It is a very complicated version of a famous English proverb!

TEXT 1

Escort the equine quadruped
To the element aquatic
Ingurgitation, it is said,
May not be automatic.

Introduction

Clarity, **order** and **language** suitable for the intended audience are three essential qualities of all explanatory writing. Any piece of writing needs to use these qualities appropriately to communicate its message to the required audience.

It is often difficult to communicate complex ideas because this involves combining unfamiliar nouns and adjectives. Using Text 1, we can illustrate this:

Word	Meaning
Quadruped	Four-legged
Equine	From the horse family

If we only know that a 'quadruped' is a four-legged animal, we might imagine that the rhyme is referring to a cat or dog. So we also need to know that 'equine' means 'from the horse family'. An 'equine quadruped' is therefore a horse. With this clue we can begin to understand the rhyme.

Development

We are now going to think about the history of the English language so that we can prepare an information sheet about this topic for Year 5 students. You may have your own class notes on this, or you could do some research in the library. To help you get started, here are some reference notes. They are not in chronological order.

a The Romans settled in Britain from 43AD to 410AD. Their Latin language left its mark mostly in place names (-chester = fort, from Latin 'castra'; straet = street or road)

b Some words were borrowed from Indian languages during the years of British rule in India (18th century–1947): (bungalow, chutney, curry, jungle, pundit, guru, verandah etc).

c The Celts, earliest recorded settlers of Britain from 500BC, left us a few words to describe the landscape (tor = peak; dun = down; crag = rock; combe = valley).

d Scientific discoveries from the eighteenth century onwards were often given names deriving from Latin or Greek, which the scientists had studied at school (antiseptic (1791); oxygen (1790); anaesthetic (1731); gene (1910); vitamin (1912); ozone (1840)). New inventions were named using Greek words: tele = far off; phonos = sound; giving us the word 'telephone')

e Vikings from Scandinavia who invaded and then settled in northern Britain from 787AD onwards left many words seen now in place names and dialect (-by = farm; -thorp = village; -twaite = isolated area).

f Christian missionaries from 600AD onwards, and church work in the Middle Ages (1066-1485) added thousands of Latin words to English (angel, school, verse, candle, history, grammar, elephant, plant, altar etc).

g The Anglo-Saxon invasions and settlements from 430AD onwards brought with them the Germanic languages that are the basis of English. The first great works of English literature were composed in Anglo-Saxon.

h The Norman invasion of 1066 brought about 10,000 French words into English. Many had to do with government, the church and the law (parliament, cathedral, saint, arrest, justice, prison, crime etc).

1 With a partner, read notes A to H above and then follow these steps:

2 Using the letters, put the paragraphs in chronological order.

3 Now, working alone, think of your young audience. How are you going to make your information clear and well-ordered? Will you write in paragraphs or set out your points as a flow chart or diagram?

4 You will not need all the detail given above. What information are you going to choose to leave in or out? Try to use some of the techniques shown in the Introduction. Don't forget to review the material in Year 7, Unit 6 on pages 19–21.

5 Rough out your ideas. Add or take away points. Then prepare the final draft. Check the spelling and sentences. Year 5 pupils need you to be a model of accuracy!

Review

In 1971, a Plain English campaign was launched in Britain. It aimed to make forms, instructions, guarantees and medical advice absolutely clear to the reader. By 1985, 21,000 such documents had been simplified and the process still continues.

In what sort of information material would Plain English be most useful to you? Make your suggestions to the class.

Character portraits

Aims

- To revise descriptive writing.
- To reconsider the methods of such writing.
- To write a description of a person.

Starter session

Think of a memorable character in a book you have read recently. On paper, write down three important things that you can remember about your character. Put up your hand and read these to the class, explaining why you find your character interesting.

Introduction

Charles Dickens (1812–70) created hundreds of memorable characters in his novels and stories. In a famous painting of him, kept at the Dickens House Museum in London, you can see him surrounded by tiny figures, some of the many people he made come alive in his writing.

The secret of Dickens's power was his sharp observation and memory of detail. He also used descriptive techniques that we can imitate ourselves when we want to describe characters.

1 Read this description of Miss Murdstone from *David Copperfield* (1849) (Text 1). David is a boy whose young widowed mother decides to remarry. Grim Mr Murdstone is her choice. He brings his equally unpleasant sister, Miss Murdstone, to live with them. The cruel step-father and his sister torment David and his mother mercilessly. This is how Miss Murdstone is described:

DAVID COPPERFIELD (extract)

It was Miss Murdstone who was arrived, and a gloom-looking lady she was; dark, like her brother, whom she greatly resembled in face and voice; and with very heavy eyebrows, nearly meeting over her large nose, as if, being disabled by the wrongs of her sex from wearing whiskers, she had carried them to that account. She brought with her, two uncompromising hard black boxes, with her initials on the lids in hard brass nails. When she paid the coachman she took her money out of a hard steel purse, and she kept the purse in a very jail of a bag which hung upon her arm by heavy chains, and shut up like a bite. I had never, at that time, seen such a metallic lady altogether as Miss Murdstone was.

She was brought into the parlour with many tokens of welcome, and there formally recognised my mother as a new and near relation. Then she looked at me, and said: 'Is that your boy, sister-in-law?'

My mother acknowledged me.

'Generally speaking', said Miss Murdstone, 'I don't like boys...'

Having uttered which, with great distinctness, she begged the favour of being shown to her room, which became to me from that time forth a place of awe and dread, wherein the two black boxes were never seen open or known to be left unlocked, and where (for I peeped in once or twice when she was out) numerous little steel fetters and rivets, with which Miss Murdstone embellished herself when she was dressed, generally hung upon the looking-glass in formidable array.

Development

You can see various methods of character creation here.

1 With a partner, answer these points:

- What two words are built into 'Murdstone', and what do they suggest?
- Find three details of her actual appearance.
- Find five well-chosen adjectives that describe her.
- Find a simile and some metaphors about her.
- Look over the description of her possessions:
  - Boxes
  - Bag
  - Jewellery.
- What are the key words in these descriptions and how do they reflect the aggression and hardness of the owner?
- What does the way she speaks tell us?
- Her room becomes like her. Which two words show David's feelings for it (and her)?

2 You are going to create your own character description, using some of the techniques noted above. Here are some ideas:

- A new teacher at a school of wizards
- An eccentric football manager of a rising team
- A runaway girl who lives rough on the city streets
- A new and strange commander of the starship 'Exploration'

Choose one of these, or invent your own character. Your analysis of Miss Murdstone will have taught you some techniques to use.

3 Working on your own, invent a name for your character that expresses her or his personality then make a star chart around that name. Add ideas on these points:

- Appearance
- Clothing and belongings
- Habits or ways of behaving
- Ways of speaking

4 Now use a thesaurus to find some really strong and expressive descriptive adjectives. Perhaps your character has a room or office that reflects her or his personality.

5 Now turn your notes into a paragraph or two. If you include speech, remember that each new speaker starts a new paragraph. When you are happy with your first draft – and you may need to add or take away details – write the final version of your description. Don't forget to proofread the final version for any mistakes.

Review

Imagine Mr Murdstone, David Copperfield's step-father. You can guess something about him form the description of his sister. Think of some similes to describe him:

- His face was as dark as ...
- His voice was like ...
- His clothes were as black as ...
- His manner was as cold as ...
- His anger was like ...

Share your ideas with the class.

A *persuasive letter*

Aims

- To look again at persuasive writing.
- To revise persuasive techniques.
- To write a persuasive letter about school uniform.

Starter session

Do you wear a school uniform? With a partner, discuss what you like and dislike about uniforms.

- How many items do you have to buy?
- How much does it all cost?
- Is it suitable and convenient for your life in school?

Write a list, and then share your ideas with the rest of the class.

Introduction

To 'persuade' means that you use language to make someone else do something or come to agree with your point of view. There are delicate effects of language ('rhetorical devices') that you can use to win over the other person. Here are some of them again:

- Repetition
- Rhetorical questions (that expect a certain answer)
- Points leading to a climax
- Well-chosen adjectives and verbs
- Use of statistics
- Slogans
- Comparisons
- Use of clear key points in an ordered structure of paragraphs
- Use of style to fit your intended audience.

Development

Imagine that you have written a letter (Text 1) to the school magazine. You hope that your persuasion will make the Headteacher consider abolishing uniform so that pupils may wear their own choice of clothes to school.

Read this letter carefully.

1 With a partner, find examples of some of the rhetorical devices used in persuasive writing listed above. Write down your chosen examples.

Dear editor

I am writing to the magazine to protest about that dreary imposition on young people: school uniform. Here are my ideas about the subject. I hope they will convince your readers to join me in my campaign to throw off the chains of uniformity, so that we can become proud, independent-minded, free students.

Which schools outside Britain have school uniform? None! I repeat, none! American high-school pupils have lovely clothes, and the European exchange students who come to our school laugh at us and think we're weird! You don't want to be the laughing stock of the Western world, do you?

Uniform costs too much money, about £150 per pupil. There are so many items to buy, they're so expensive and they're so badly made. Last year I had to have two pullovers because the elbows wore through! All those badges make things hard to wash. The worst things are ties. Who wears ties these days? My dad works in a large company. You hardly see a tie in the office and they have a wonderful idea called 'dress down Friday' when employees can wear casual clothes. The company doesn't stop being successful!

Why do we have a uniform to make us all look the same? Education is meant to make us individuals, isn't it? We look like the workers in George Orwell's '1984' or those slaves in the 'Metropolis' film we saw in English.

Set us free! Uniform is dull, it's expensive, it doesn't last, it stops us growing up and, above all, it prevents us being individuals! Get rid of uniform!

Yours sincerely

Indignant pupil

2 You are now going to write the Head's reply to the magazine. She/he wants to persuade the young audience that uniform is a good thing for a school.

With a partner, make two lists:
- the benefits of uniform,
- answers to the points made in 'Indignant's' letter.

3 Now, working alone, prepare a structure for your answer. 'Indignant' had three main points, with an introduction and conclusion. Use the same pattern. Choose your three points. Add evidence to each.

Here are some starters:
- Rich pupils would show off with designer clothes
- Uniform gives you pride in your school
- It's nicer to save your best clothes for the weekend.

4 Now think about style. The Headteacher is formal but writing for a young audience. Where can you use rhetorical devices? Add these as you write your first draft. Remember to answer some of the objections made by 'Indignant' (for example: some of last year's pullovers were badly made so you have now changed to a new and better supplier).

5 Write the final draft of the letter. You are the Headteacher so check it very carefully for punctuation, spelling and sentence structure.

Review

Look at some letters in magazines and newspapers. Can you spot the ones that are writing to persuade? Which ones are the most persuasive and why? Share your ideas with the class.

Developing arguments

Aims

- To revise writing to argue.
- To explore how to develop and signpost an argument.
- To write an argument about the timing of the school day.

Starter session

At Sunnyhill Community School, the day starts at 9.00am and finishes at 3.30pm. There is an hour for lunch. The governors want to change to a 'continental' day, which would start at 8.00am, have no lunch break and finish at 1.00pm. Some of the teachers, parents and students think this would be a good idea; some do not.

Using the first person, write down what the following people might think:

- Mr Stevens, teacher, travels 30 miles to and from school each day
- Jonathan, Year 11 student, has a job in a local shop in the evening
- Louise, Year 8 student, has a morning paper round
- Mrs Thompson, single parent of Year 7 student, works full time
- Manesh, Year 9 student, enjoys football in his spare time
- Miss Higginson, drama teacher, runs an after-school drama club.

Offer your ideas to the rest of the class.

Introduction

With a partner, make lists of points for and against the idea of changing the school day. Here are some ideas to stimulate your thinking:

- On dark winter mornings, pupils going to school at 8am would have more accidents.
- Homework could be done more efficiently in the afternoon, allowing pupils a free evening.
- Vandalism and petty crime might increase if pupils were free in the afternoon.
- More sport and school activities would take place after 1pm.
- Too many pupils would be 'home alone' because parents are working.

Development

1 Working alone, practise some of the techniques you can use in your argument. Use some 'rhetorical devices' (see Year 8, Unit 8, p.63).

Here are some further techniques to develop and signpost your argument:

Technique	Example	Your example
Third person	Many people think.	
Connectives	However,....	
Present tense	Many students agree with....	
Phrases that introduce evidence	As evidence of this..	
Phrases that link paragraphs	On the other hand,...	
Clause which show a conclusion	It can therefore be seen that...	

2 Take your rough notes and consider your points for and against. Now choose <u>one side</u>. Do you want to change the day or not?

3 Select the four most important points from your list. These are now the basis for four paragraphs. Now develop the evidence for each point.

4 Write a draft of your article. Try to include some rhetorical devices and some of the techniques noted above. Check and correct it carefully when you complete it for homework.

5 Present your article to the rest of the class.

Review

Look back over your lists of points for and against changing the day. Which single idea seems to you the most forceful? Read it to the class. Someone should answer you.

Problem page

Aims

- To look again at writing intended to advise us.
- To revise and develop the technoques and qualities of advice writing.
- To write letters of advice from an 'agony aunt'.

Starter session

Remind yourself of the meaning of 'advise' and its difference from 'instruct'. You obviously get lots of good advice in school. From where, outside school, does useful advice come to you? Write down a list of sources.

> ### INFORMATION
>
> **advise/advice** – 'advise' is the verb; 'advice' is the noun

Introduction

Here are some reminders about advice writing:
- You need to know the audience it is aimed at
- Its style and tone should fit that audience
- It needs to be clear
- A heading point, backed up by further evidence, makes a good advice paragraph
- Plain words and straightforward sentences are most suitable
- Good presentation helps to put across the message.

With a partner, discuss why good advice – about smoking, doing homework at a sensible time, eating fruit and vegetables, not going late to bed, for example – is so often ignored.

Development

1 As a class, discuss these points:
- What are 'agony aunts'? Where do you find their advice?
- On what kind of subjects do they give us advice? Do they serve a useful function?

2 Read the following 'problem page' letter from a young reader of a teenage magazine:

Dear Agony Aunt,

My best friend and I have been together since Infant School. We have always sat together in lessons and have gone out together at weekends and during school holidays. However, she has now started going out with a boy in our class and she wants to spend all her time with him. I feel very lonely and I am often left out as everyone else in the class has got their own friendships. I hate going to school now because I am always on my own.

Yours sincerely,
Lonely (Glasgow)

3 With a partner, make notes on how you would answer this letter. Think of three main points of advice to offer the letter writer. Then make notes on evidence to back each point.

For example:
- You should speak to your friend
- You should try new activities
- You should try and make new friends.

4 Now, working alone, take your plan and write up each paragraph. Remember to make the style plain and clear to help the young reader take in your advice quickly. Friendship problems have no easy answers. How are you going to start and end your letter sympathetically?

5 Check your final draft against the criteria for advice writing suggested in the Introduction.

Review

Think again about 'agony aunts'. Do they influence girls more than boys? Why is that? What sort of qualities would you want in an 'agony aunt' for boys? Put your ideas to the class.

Animal rights

Aims

- To look again at writing to analyse.
- To remind ourselves of how this writing works.
- To write a report based on evidence relating to a factory farm.

Starter session

In pairs, think of five reasons why homework is a bad thing and five reasons why it is good.

To reach a conclusion, you would have to analyse these reasons: that is, look at the ideas in detail so that you can understand them and then reach a decision.

Analyse your two lists. Which is more convincing and would therefore win the argument?

Introduction

The situation:
Sunnyhill Poultry Farm is situated just outside the village of Sunnyhill. A 'factory farm', owned by the Taylor family, it has been there for twenty years.

Recently the factory has been extended and was heavily criticised by the local community for taking over a field which had been tipped as the location for a new local children's playground.

Concerned about the outcry from the village and in order to restore its reputation, the Taylor family financed and constructed an adventure playground nearer the centre of the village. This allowed the council to use its limited funds elsewhere.

HINTS!

When writing to analyse, you have to look at evidence methodically, thinking about it in an orderly way in detail and looking at every point, even minor ones. You must take into account the opinions of people with different values, beliefs and interests.

Here is a scenario to analyse. It contains arguments covering a range of perspectives. Read through them and decide who is right. Make sure you can justify your decision with evidence.

A week ago, local protesters broke into the factory and set free all the chickens and pigs. A lot of equipment was damaged in the process.

Four people were interviewed for the local newspaper. Their comments are recorded here. Read and analyse them carefully. You are going to decide which side convinces you more.

'These protesters have caused more trouble than anyone could have anticipated. These chickens and pigs are not used to living in the wild and fending for themselves so they will certainly die. There are many foxes in these parts that will undoubtedly hunt them. The problems are just beginning. We are very disappointed that this has happened to us. We have poured a lot of our profits back into this community over the years. Everybody in the village has benefited from our generosity. We have provided employment for many people. The new factory would offer even more.'

John Taylor, Farmer

Phyllis Green,
animal rights protestor

'All we have done is to liberate innocent creatures which were being kept in squalor – conditions which no living creature should have to endure. Cruelty to animals, testing and experimentation are barbaric and should not be tolerated in a civilised society. The Taylors deserve all that is coming to them. This is no way to produce food for humans. Vegetarianism is better and kinder.'

'These protesters should not be allowed to get away with such an outrage. We don't want to hurt living creatures but we need to experiment on animals to find cures for life-threatening diseases. Old-fashioned cruelty may have been common in medieval times, but these protesters are out of date. They are slowing down the advancement of science with these mindless acts of violence. They have attacked our labs near Sunnyhill and now they're interfering with our food supply. Farmers and scientists have to use animals to improve the quality of human life.'

Stephen Marchmont,
scientist at nearby
research laboratory

'Well! I'm thrilled that somebody has finally put a stop to the foul smells and noise which come from that factory. I dread to think what cruelty goes on in those cramped cages. At least for a while there will be no more lorries clunking around at all hours of the day and night. The way that family got away with building on the site of a potential playground was criminal. The one they plan to build is too far away from the houses and too near a main road. Local children should come before individual profit. What the protesters did is an absolute triumph! I hope the pigs and hens find happier lives away from Sunnyhill.'

Claire Forsythe, local resident

Development

1 As a class, read over the four interviews.

2 Now, working with a partner, analyse each person's statements. You might try to group your points under headings for and against the new factory. Which side seems more convincing to you?

3 Working alone, imagine that you are on the local council. You are going to write a report for the Chairman of the council.

- You will need to explain the various opinions.
- Four paragraphs would be best, with two describing the support and two about the opposition.
- You can end by recommending one side of the argument to help the council in its decision making.

4 Write the final report. Check its accuracy and technical detail carefully. You want to impress the Chairman!

Review

As a class, think about the difficulty of the council Chairman's decision. Divide into those who support the protesters and those who are against. One volunteer from each side should present three points of evidence. Then take a class vote.

Book review

Aims

- To study writing to review.
- To reconsider the nature and qualities of such writing.
- To write a detailed book review.

Starter session

Think about these points with a partner:

- How and where can you find out about books that you might want to read?
- When you look at a book, how can you get a brief idea of its contents?
- Where would you find actual book reviews?

Share your ideas with the class.

Introduction

A good fiction review should give you information about a book and stimulate you to read it. A well-balanced review is made of several elements:

- The **facts**: title; author; date of first publication; publisher; film or TV versions; any other striking fact that you can find.
- A brief **summary** of what the book is about.
- The **setting**: the place or time in which the events of the book take place.
- **Characterisation**: concise points on some of the main characters. Who are they? Why are they interesting? How do they impact on each other?
- **Theme**: a general idea behind the book. For example, the theme of Dickens's *Oliver Twist* (1837) is the harshness and cruelty of the nineteenth-century workhouse system. Not all books have a theme.
- What are the **strengths** of the book? Some brief quotations might be useful.
- What are its **weaknesses**?
- **Final verdict**. What do you think of the book overall? What do other critics think (you sometimes see quotations on the back cover)?
- For what **age group** and **audience** would you recommend it?

Development

You are now going to write a one-page review of a book you have read recently, either in class or on your own.

Sometimes it is fun to have a dramatic opening paragraph to catch the reader's imagination. It might say a few exciting things about the book:

For example:

'The bleak, sinister hills of Dartmoor; an ancient mansion shadowed by fear; a centuries old family curse; a huge, terrifying ghostly Hound whose howls echo at midnight; a great detective who has defeated master criminals but who now meets his match in facing the supernatural: these are the elements of Arthur Conan Doyle's greatest Sherlock Holmes story: *The Hound of the Baskervilles.*'

1 What would you choose from your book to make such an opening?

2 To prepare the subsequent paragraphs, start with a list of numbered points. You may not need all the ideas noted in the Introduction.

3 Under your headings, jot down more detailed notes about the characters (age, appearance, background, for example). Then:
   - Check details from the book itself, if you can
   - If you are including quotations, find and copy them from the text. Do not make them too long. Remember to put inverted commas around them.

4 Imagine that your review is for a children's book magazine. The audience consists of young readers like yourself. Keep the style clear and exciting. You want your readers to share your enjoyment of the book.

5 When you are satisfied with your notes, write a draft.

Review

Run a quick class election for the most popular book. Suggest some titles. List these on the board. Then vote on them for a winner.

Narratorial devices

Aims

- To look again at storytelling in writing.
- To examine the role of the narrator.
- To write a short scene from different narrator viewpoints.

Starter session

In some novels, the story is told by the author; in others, the narrator is one of the characters.

- Remind yourself of the advantages of each method.
- Which do you prefer, and why?
- After making brief notes, compare your answers and see if there is any preference in the class.

Introduction

Jane Eyre (1847) is Charlotte Brontë's most famous novel.

In it, eighteen-year-old Jane is appointed governess at the mysterious Thornfield Hall in Yorkshire. Strange and sinister laughter is heard coming from the supposedly unused rooms at the top of the house. Jane and her employer, the powerful Mr Rochester, fall in love. They plan to be married very quietly in the local church.

1 Read Text 1 from the novel. Jane is the narrator.

2 With a partner, discuss the narrative power of this passage.

- Which phrases in the opening sentence suggest Jane's calm, unsuspecting mood?
- How do the strangers become more and more threatening as the passage continues?
- When the impediment (something that blocks the way) is declared, why are the adjectives 'distinct' and 'near' so powerful?
- How exactly does Mr. Rochester respond to the interruption?

- How do the adverbs 'distinctly', 'calmly', 'steadily' and 'not loudly' contribute to the force of the conclusion?
- How does the narrative hold back the final revelation of the hidden message?

3 Make brief notes and share your points with the class.

TEXT **1**

JANE EYRE (extract)

And now I can recall the picture of the old gray house of God rising calm before me, of a rook wheeling round the steeple, of a ruddy morning sky beyond. I remember something, too, of the green grave-mounds; and I have not forgotten, either, two figures of strangers straying among the low hillocks and reading the momentoes graven on the few mossy headstones.[…]

We entered the quiet and humble temple; the priest waited in his white surplice at the lowly altar, the clerk beside him. All was still: two shadows only moved in a remote corner.[…]

Our place was taken at the communion rails. Hearing a cautious step behind me, I glanced over my shoulder: one of the strangers – a gentleman, evidently – was advancing up the chancel. The service began. The explanation of the intent of matrimony was gone through; and then the clergyman came a step farther forward, and, bending slightly towards Mr. Rochester, went on:

'I require and charge you both (as ye will answer at the dreadful Day of Judgement when the secrets of all hearts shall be disclosed), that if either of you know any impediment why ye may not lawfully be joined together in matrimony, ye do now confess it'.[…]

He paused, as the custom is. When is the pause after that sentence ever broken by reply? Not perhaps, once in a hundred years. And the clergyman, who had not lifted his eyes from his book, and had held his breath but for a moment, was proceeding: his hand was already stretched towards Mr. Rochester, as his lips unclosed to ask, 'Wilt thou have this woman for thy wedded wife?' – when a distinct and near voice said –

'The marriage cannot go on: I declare the existence of an impediment.'

The clergyman looked up at the speaker and stood mute; the clerk did the same; Mr. Rochester moved slightly, as if an earthquake had rolled under his feet: taking a firmer footing, and not turning his head or eyes, he said, 'Proceed.'

Profound silence fell when he uttered that word, with deep but low intonation.[…]

Mr. Wood seemed at a loss. 'What is the nature of the impediment?' he asked. 'Perhaps it may be got over – explained away?'

'Hardly,' was the answer. 'I have called it insuperable, and I speak advisedly.'

The speaker came forward and leaned on the rails. He continued, uttering each word distinctly, calmly, steadily, but not loudly –

'It simply consists in the existence of a previous marriage. Mr. Rochester has a wife now living.'

Development

The strangers are a Mr. Mason and his lawyer. They declare that Mr. Rochester is already married to Mason's sister, Bertha. He was tricked into marriage, her growing insanity having been hidden from him. He has kept his tragic, often violent wife locked away at Thornfield for years. He hoped for happiness with a new, young bride.

1 Using the background details below, imagine the scene narrated from the viewpoint of:
- Mr Mason
- Mr Rochester

Richard Mason (background):

As a young man, Rochester met Mason in Jamaica, where the Masons ran a plantation. Mason is a cowardly man who is always cold, as he suffers from tropical fevers. He is determined to stop Rochester marrying again. He is too weak to speak to Rochester directly and lets his lawyer do the talking.

Edward Rochester (background):

Rochester's marriage soon declined into a living hell. He took his insane wife to England and kept her locked away, but carefully looked after, at Thornfield. He thinks he has found a true wife in Jane, with her intelligence, honesty and beauty. He believes his first marriage was a sham and that he is right to marry Jane.

2 Working alone, make rough notes on the two viewpoints:
For <u>Mason</u>, include:
- His wish to hide in the background
- His thoughts about his unfortunate sister
- His observations of Jane
- His fear of Rochester and his possible reactions to the intervention.

For <u>Rochester</u>, include:
- His awareness of the strangers
- His recognition of Mason
- His guilt about his first wife
- His concern and love for Jane
- His horror at the intervention and the revelation of his dark secret.

3 Then turn your notes into sentences and paragraphs. Here are some possible openings:

<u>Mason</u>

I was shivering with cold and nerves as I hung about the dismal churchyard, pretending to look at the graves. Then I saw them approaching...

<u>Rochester</u>

I felt calm and happy as Jane and I walked together towards the old church where so many of my ancestors had been married and were buried in their marble tombs...

Include all the events of the passage. Make sure that any speech is properly punctuated and is set out correctly.

Review

Jane Austen (1775–1817) always told her stories from a woman's viewpoint. In her modern ghost story, *The Woman in Black*, Susan Hill, the contemporary novelist, uses a male narrator.

- Is it possible for a male author to write through a woman's eyes, or for a woman writer to narrate through the eyes of a man?

Share your thoughts on this with the class.

YEAR **9** **UNIT 2**

The First World War

Aims

- To compare factual and imaginative writing.
- To study letters and a poem from First World War writing.
- To write two imaginative letters about trench warfare.

Starter session

Theodore Wilson was a schoolmaster who volunteered to serve in the First World War (1914–18). A brave officer, he was killed on 23 March 1918. Like many young soldiers of the time, he wrote poems about his experience of war. Here is part of '**France, 1917**', describing the terrible Western Front.

 TEXT **1**

FRANCE, 1917 (extract)

'Old wire crept through the grass there like a snake,
Orange-red in the sunlight, cruel as lust.
And a dead hand groped up blindly from the mould...
A dandelion flamed through ribs – like a heart of gold,
And a stink of rotten flesh came up from the dust...
With a twinkle of little wings against the sun
A lark praised God for all that he had done.

There was nothing here that moved but a lonely bird,
And the wind over the grass. Men lived in mud;
Slept as their dead must sleep, walled in with clay,
Yet staring out across the unpitying day,
Staring hard-eyed like hawks that hope for blood.
The still land was a witch who held her breath,
And with a lidless eye kept watch for death.'

Vocabulary

old wire: barbed wire defences

in mud: in the trenches

Wilson gives us graphic details of the trench landscape and the soldiers, living and dead. He uses comparisons (similes and metaphors) to help us imagine what he has seen. With a partner, find these. What is compared to what in them? Make quick notes and discuss them as a class.

Introduction

Civilians in Britain had very little idea of the nature of trench warfare on the Western Front in France and Belgium. There was no television news, and film and photography were heavily censored. Yet men could describe what they had seen and felt in letters home. Usually, horrors were kept from families, but male friends or fellow soldiers might be told more.

1 As a class, read these passages from letters written by soldiers. Almost all of these men were killed in the war.

> Tomorrow I shall take my men over the top to do our bit in the first attack...I could not wish for a finer death; and you will know that I died doing my duty to my God, my Country and my King.(July 1916)

> It is hideously exasperating to hear people talking the glib commonplaces about the war. Perhaps you are tempted to give them a picture of a leprous earth, scattered with the swollen and blackening corpses of hundreds of young men. The appalling stench of rotting carrion...Mud like porridge, trenches like shallow and sloping cracks in the porridge – porridge that stinks in the sun. Swarms of flies and bluebottles... Men with bowels dropping out, lungs shot away, with blinded smashed faces...Men screaming and gibbering. Wounded men hanging in agony on the barbed wire, until a friendly spurt of liquid fire shrivels them up like a fly in a candle...(June 1917)

> Tomorrow we go over the top. I pray that I may be worthy of my fighting ancestors...The spirit of the Brigade of Guards will carry all resistance before it. The pride of being such a regiment. I have never been prouder of anything, except your love for me, than I am of being a Grenadier. (September 1916)

> A misty summer morning – no sign of humanity – a dead land. And yet thousands of men were there, like rabbits concealed... Then, as a rabbit in the early morning comes out to crop grass, a German stepped over the enemy trench... 'I'll take him,' says the man near me. And like a rabbit the German falls. And again complete silence and desolation. (1915)

2 Now look closely at the letters with a partner.

- What sort of audience does each letter have?
- Some strike brave attitudes – and the courage of these men was extraordinary. What are they proud of as they prepare to die in a battle offensive? What is left out of their letters?
- Others are concerned with the harsh realities of war. What exactly are the horrors that they describe? How do these writers use:
  - Forceful adjectives
  - Shocking comparisons (remember to look at 'leprous', for example)
  - Sensory details?

3 What do you admire about the letters?

Development

You are now going to use your imagination, and facts taken from the soldiers' writing above, to write **two** letters from a First World War soldier.

- It is 30 July 1916.
- The mighty Battle of the Somme is about to begin and you are to be in the first day's attacks.

1 The **first** letter is to your family, telling them of your hopes to fight bravely and your pride in the Cause.

- It is likely to be in rather abstract, heroic-sounding language. You avoid the horrors, and think of courage and sacrifice. This will be a short letter of one or two paragraphs.

2 The **second** is to a brother or male friend. You can speak frankly to him, detailing the horrors you have experienced.

- It will be in plain, straightforward language, sometimes angry in tone.
- Remember those deadly adjectives and forceful verbs, and the comparisons.
- It will be mostly description but there may be a short narrative about the death of a comrade.
- You can write more here: three to four paragraphs.

3 Head both letters:

On active service
30 June 1916

4 Here are some other images that you may want to bear in mind:

lice   rats   barbed wire   No man's land (between the trench lines)

shell bursts   snipers' bullets   poppies on the trench parapet

a colourless, mud-walled world   hiss of bullets and scream of shells

Review

Here are two more verses from Theodore Wilson's poem:

TEXT **2**

FRANCE, 1917 (continued)

'The guns were there in the green and wounded wild,
Hurling death as a boy may throw a stone.
And the man who served them, with unquickened breath,
Dealt, like a grocer, with their pounds of death.
Thunderous over the fields their iron was thrown,
And beyond the horizon men who could laugh and feel
Lay in the wet dust, red from brow to heel.

The bodies of men lay down in the dark of the earth:
Young flesh, through which life shines a friendly flame,
Was crumbled green in the fingers of decay...
Among the last year's oats and thistles lay
A forgotten boy, who hid as though in shame
A face that the rats had eaten...Thistle seeds
Danced daintily above the rebel weeds.'

- Discuss what you find impressive or memorable about these lines.
- They are full of contrasts. What are these?
- Are these two verses better than those printed in the Starter session above?
- You may include some of these extra ideas in your letters.

The best things

Aims

- To look again at writing used to explore feelings and ideas.
- To study diction, imagery and structure in a Rupert Brooke poem.
- To write a personal response imitating the poem.

Starter session

Life offers us many expensive pleasures, such as exotic holidays, glamorous cars, designer clothes, beautiful jewellery...

Yet there are countless simple pleasures that cost nothing, such as a splendid sunset, the spring flowers appearing, a rainbow, your mother's smile...

In rough, make a list of ten of these simple, free pleasures. Then compare notes with a partner.

Introduction

Many poets have reflected on the simple things in life. One was Rupert Brooke (1887–1915).

Brooke wrote '**The Great Lover**' (Text 1) in 1914. His title is sarcastic: he is not writing about the joys and problems of human love, but about the simple things he enjoys in his life. Text 1 is part of the poem.

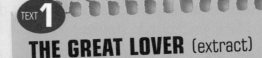

TEXT **1**

THE GREAT LOVER (extract)

These I have loved:
White plates and cups, clean-gleaming,
Ringed with blue lines; and feathery, faery dust;
Wet roofs, beneath the lamp-light; the strong crust
Of friendly bread; and many-tasting food;
Rainbows; and the blue bitter smoke of wood;

And radiant raindrops couching in cool flowers;
And flowers themselves, that sway through sunny hours,
Dreaming of moths that drink them under the moon.
Then, the cool kindliness of sheets, that soon
Smooth away trouble; and the rough male kiss
Of blankets; grainy wood; live hair that is
Shining and free; blue-massing clouds; the keen
Unpassioned beauty of a great machine;
The benison of hot water; furs to touch;
The good smell of old clothes; and other such –
The comfortable smell of friendly fingers,
Hair's fragrance, and the musty reek that lingers
About dead leaves and last year's ferns […]

- Brooke uses a rough **pentameter** (five beats to the line):

  u / u / u / u / u /
  Wet roofs, beneath the lamp-light; the strong crust

  The syllables marked 'u' are unstressed, those marked '/' are stressed. This is a very common form of poetic writing.

- The lines are **rhyming couplets** (dust/crust; flowers/hours etc)

1 The poem takes the form of a list with items divided by semi-colons. With a partner, look at:

   - The simple things Brooke loves
   - The methods he uses to define them.

2 With which items do you agree? With which do you disagree? Which seem old-fashioned or just strange?

3 Some items are single words: rainbows, furs; others have delicately chosen adjectives to define them. List some of the adjectives that you find particularly effective.

4 Some items involve metaphors (indirect comparisons). Which are these?

5 Brooke uses details observed through his senses in defining his pleasures. Which senses are used for which items?

Development

You can explore the idea of simple pleasures in your own writing.

1 Look back at the list of ten free things that give you pleasure from the Starter session. Some of these may be the same as Brooke's.

   However, it is 90 years since Brooke was writing, so do not forget up-to-date ideas: the noise your computer makes as an email arrives; the last minute goal to win the great match.

   Remember, too, personal things about people that you love, and pets, or favourite kinds of weather: Brooke is silent on these.

2 You are going to write your own poem entitled 'Life's Simple Pleasures'. With a partner, read over your lists. You may inspire each other with fresh ideas.

3 Now think about defining some of the ideas more closely using:
   - Adjectives (especially colours)
   - Comparisons (similes or metaphors)
   - Full sentences (as Brooke used in his 'flowers' lines).

4 You are ready to write a full draft. Start:

> LIFE'S SIMPLE PLEASURES
>
> These are the things that I love:

   - If you feel that you can handle rhyme and pentameter like Brooke, do so (but do not distort your meaning in the struggle).
   - Otherwise write in what might be called 'heightened prose', making a list of items, some short, some long, divided by semi-colons.
   - Define each item carefully to bring it alive.

5 Check the wording when you finish, especially the adjectives and comparisons: are they sharp and fresh enough?

Review

Your teacher will ask some of you to read your poems to the class. Make notes on the strengths and weaknesses of each one and decide which you think is best. Why? Is it because of the sound of the words used, or because of the ideas in the poem?

Ghost stories

Aims

- To look at the ghost story as written entertainment.
- To consider the creation of atmosphere and tension in such a story.
- To write part of a ghost story.

Starter session

Charles Dickens (1812–70) loved ghost stories and wrote some excellent examples of the genre, notably *A Christmas Carol* (1843) and *The Signalman* (1866). Text 1 is part of his story, '**The Haunted House**' (1859):

TEXT **1**

THE HAUNTED HOUSE (extract)

It was a solitary house, standing in a sadly neglected garden.[...] It was uninhabited, but had, within a year or two, been cheaply repaired to render it habitable; I say cheaply, because the work had been done in a surface manner, and was already decaying as to the paint and plaster.[...] A lop-sided board drooped over the garden wall, announcing that it was 'to let on very reasonable terms, well furnished.' It was much too closely and heavily shadowed by trees, and, in particular, there were six tall poplars before the front windows, which were excessively melancholy.[...]
It was easy to see that it was an avoided house – a house that nobody would take. And the natural inference was, that it had the reputation of being a haunted house.[...]

> **Vocabulary**
>
> *melancholy* – sad
>
> *inference* – conclusion

- Read this passage with a partner. Dickens, in masterly style, makes us see the house as sinister and frightening. Find the adjectives and adverbs which create this effect.

Introduction

Victorian readers were very fond of ghost stories. As there were no films, television or radio in the nineteenth century, their ghostly thrills came from reading.

Mary Elizabeth Braddon (1835–1915) wrote Text 2 **'The Shadow in the Corner'** for Dickens's *All the Year Round* magazine in 1879.

● Read these extracts from the story.

BACKGROUND

Michael Bascom, an elderly scientist, lives in an isolated house 'given over to rats and mice, loneliness, echoes...' He spends his time on scientific research. Local tradition says that one of his ancestors killed himself in an attic room of the house. When a maid complains of dreadful dreams when she sleeps in that room, Bascom determines to spend the night there to prove that it is not haunted.

Vocabulary

diabolical – devilish

TEXT **2**

THE SHADOW IN THE CORNER
(extract)

The old clock on the stairs was striking two as Michael slowly ascended, candle in hand, to the hitherto unknown region of the attics. At the top of the staircase he found himself facing a dark narrow passage which led northwards, a passage that was in itself sufficient to strike terror to a superstitious mind, so black and uncanny did it look.[…]

He opened the door of the north room, and stood looking about him. It was a large room, with a ceiling that sloped on one side, but was fairly lofty upon the other; an old-fashioned room, full of old-fashioned furniture associated with a day that was gone and people that were dead. A walnut-wood wardrobe stared him in the face – a wardrobe with brass handles, which gleamed out of the darkness like diabolical eyes. There was a tall four-post bedstead, which had been cut down one side to accommodate the slope of the ceiling, and which had a misshapen and deformed aspect in consequence. There was an old mahogany bureau, that smelt of secrets.[…]

'It is a dismal room', mused Michael.[…]

'Atmosphere' in writing means the mood conveyed by a place.

- With a partner, read over the passage and pick out the words, comparisons and phrases that suggest the horror of the passage and the room.

TEXT 3

THE SHADOW IN THE CORNER

(extract 2)

The first streak of light crept in at the window – dim, and cold, and grey; then came twilight, and he looked at the corner between the wardrobe and the door. Yes; there was the shadow: not the shadow of the wardrobe only – that was clear enough, but a vague and shapeless something which darkened the dull brown wall; so faint, so shadowy, that he could form no conjecture as to its nature, or the thing it represented.[...]

BACKGROUND

Bascom tries to sleep but seems to be possessed by the despairing mind of his ancestor, the suicide. Just before dawn, he sees something in the room, the shadow that the maid had feared.

Vocabulary

conjecture – guess

Ghosts in stories are more frightening when they are vague. The author mixes the half light and the shadow cleverly to suggest a horror.

- With your partner, pick out the words here which describe the twilight and the ghostly form half seen.

There are more grim twists to the story as Bascom is at last forced to believe in the supernatural. You can read it all in *The Oxford book of English ghost stories* (1986).

Development

1 Try writing a passage from a ghost story. It should contain two things:

- An atmospheric setting that builds up a frightening mood
- A glimpse of the ghost itself.

Do not write the whole story. Concentrate on your writing skill to produce the mood, as Dickens and Mary Braddon do in the passages above.

Here are some situations, taken from famous ghost stories, that might inspire you:

- You are in the beautiful park of a large country house on a hot, still afternoon, when you look up and see a dark, threatening figure looking down at you from the battlemented roof of the house...(*The Turn of the Screw* by Henry James)
- You are walking along a deserted, cold, wind-swept beach at twilight, when you look behind and see a strange being in fluttering garments feverishly pursuing you... (*Oh, Whistle and I'll Come to You* by M.R. James)
- You have broken into an empty, locked up house on a hot afternoon. Then you hear something moving upstairs, a thing that hops, and then scratches its nails along the bedroom doors...(*The Clock* by W.F. Harvey)
- You have a bet with a friend that you can spend a night in the haunted Red Room of an old castle. You enter the room and light many candles. Then they mysteriously begin to go out...(*The Red Room* by H.G. Wells)
- You have gone to a strange, empty, isolated house on an island just off the coast. You explore the nearby graveyard at twilight. Then you see her: a woman, deathly pale, dressed in black, old-fashioned clothes...(*The Woman in Black* by Susan Hill)

2 Make rough notes for your scene. Remember that you can create atmosphere in describing a setting by:

- Use of details observed through your senses
- Vivid adjectives
- Well-chosen adverbs and verbs
- A few apt comparisons.

Suggest the ghost delicately, as Mary Braddon does. Something half-seen is more fearful than obvious rattling chains and heads tucked under arms!

3 Write your final draft in two or three paragraphs.

Review

Many films try to thrill us with supernatural stories full of special effects. Can you think of the titles of any such films that you have seen? How exactly does the film-maker create atmosphere and shock? Which is more effective in thrilling us: words or film effects? Make quick notes and discuss as a class.

Home town

Aims

- To reconsider writing to inform.
- To revise selection and presentation of information.
- To write an information guide to the place where you live.

Starter session

Imagine you are looking for a new place to live. What are the most important factors in choosing a new town or village or city?

Working on your own, make quick notes. Then discuss your conclusions with the class.

Introduction

The qualities of a good piece of information writing include:

> clarity   order   selection   useful examples
>
> right tone and language for intended audience

Here is a very brief guide to Cambridge intended for young foreign student visitors of your own age. Read it through.

WELCOME TO CAMBRIDGE

- Cambridge is one of the most exciting and beautiful small cities in Britain.
- It is often spoken of as TOWN (the city itself) and GOWN (the world famous University that dominates the city centre).
- The city is full of historic contrasts: very old houses and churches near the bridge, the many wonderful buildings of the University's colleges; and the new science parks just outside the city.
- The city centre has fine shops, especially for clothes and books, and a lively market.
- It is easy to hire a bike to explore the delightful countryside near Cambridge.
- The open-top tourist bus is exciting. It lets you see and, through a guide, hear about the sights clearly.
- Some very good post offices and an internet 'cafe' will keep you in touch with home.
- There are fast and frequent train and bus services to London and its airports.

ENJOY YOUR STAY!

1 Consider this guide with a partner. If you were a young foreign visitor, would you find:
- The order useful?
- The language suitable?
- The content appropriate?

2 Are there any other aspects of the city that you would want to know about?

Development

1 Plan a similar guide for the area where you live. Remember, you are trying to 'sell' the area, so highlight things of special interest.

First, with a partner, make rough notes, perhaps as a star-chart. Put in:
- Interesting features of your village, town or city ● Local historic sites
- Travel by train, bus or bike ● Local activities ● Entertainment
- Places to explore in the surrounding area ● Shops
- Sports' clubs or local teams ● Special traditions or festivals

2 Now, working alone, turn this plan into short paragraphs, each containing two or three sentences. Each should have a key word heading or bullet point to signpost the text for the reader.

3 When you have done a draft, look carefully at the **wording**. Your young foreign audience may find long or slang words difficult to follow. Make the language straightforward. Explain any problem words.

4 The **presentation** should be attractive: ICT would be effective here. Some illustration - a picture or two, or a map - would be helpful.

5 Finally, consider the **tone**. If you use words like 'boring' or sentences like 'There's not much to do', your visitors are going to lose interest! Be positive and encouraging about them coming to your part of the world.

Review

Think about your home area. How could it be improved? Discuss some practical ways to make life better for local people.

Diaries and journals

Aims

- To revise writing to describe.
- To look again at techniques of description.
- To consider description in diary writing.

Starter session

In 1804, William Wordsworth (1770–1850) wrote a poem about wild daffodils that he had seen by Ullswater in the Lake District. Here is part of it:

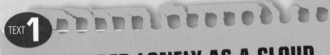

TEXT 1

I WANDERED LONELY AS A CLOUD

(extract)

I wandered lonely as a cloud
That floats on high o'er vales and hills,
When all at once I saw a crowd,
A host of golden daffodils;
Beside the lake, beneath the trees,
Fluttering and dancing in the breeze.
Continuous as the stars that shine
And twinkle on the milky way,
They stretched in never-ending line
Along the margin of a bay:
Ten thousand saw I at a glance,
Tossing their heads in sprightly dance.
The waves beside them danced; but they
Out-did the sparkling waves in glee.

Wordsworth wanted to describe what the daffodils looked like and where they were. He used two favourite descriptive techniques:

- **Comparisons**: simile (direct comparison); metaphor (indirect or suggested comparison)
- Well-chosen **adjectives** and **verbs**. With a partner, find examples of these in the poem extract.

Introduction

Wordsworth's poem was partly inspired by the **journal** (diary) of his sister Dorothy. She was an excellent descriptive writer of the natural world, and William often used her journal as the basis for his poems. Here is an extract from her journal.

JOURNAL (extract)

Thursday 15th. It was a threatening misty morning – but mild. We set off after dinner.[…] The wind was furious and we thought we must have returned. We first rested in the large boat-house, then under a furze bush.[…] Saw the plough going in the field. The wind seized our breath the lake was rough. There was a boat by itself floating in the middle of the bay.[…] When we were in the woods beyond Gowbarrow park we saw a few daffodils close to the water-side. We fancied that the lake had floated the seeds ashore and that the little colony had so sprung up. But as we went along there were more and yet more and at last under the boughs of the trees, we saw that there was a long belt of them along the shore, about the breadth of a country turnpike road. I never saw daffodils so beautiful, they grew among the mossy stones about and about them, some rested their heads upon these stones as on a pillow for weariness and the rest tossed and reeled and danced and seemed as if they verily laughed with the wind that blew upon them over the lake, they looked so gay ever glancing ever changing. This wind blew directly over the lake to them…

Development

1 With a partner, look for these features of good descriptive writing:
   - Sharply observed details
   - Similes
   - An extended metaphor
   - Sensory detail (which senses does she use the most?)
   - Use of colours
   - Precise choice of adjectives and verbs.

2 Now look again at the William's poem, written two years later. Which words and ideas has he borrowed from Dorothy's entry? Which comparisons has he invented himself? What is the obvious (and strangest) difference between the two texts?

Dorothy and William wrote about an experience that impressed them. Think of an experience of your own, for example:

- An episode from a holiday or school trip • A city walk • Out at night
- A visit to a theme park • An afternoon in the countryside
- On the beach • A quiet time in your garden, or your own room.

3 You are going to write about this experience as an entry in a journal. The audience will be yourself, and perhaps your family and close friends. You need not be too formal, therefore, but do not be as casual with your sentences as Dorothy is at times! The emphasis should be on vivid descriptive writing that will recreate your experience in words.

4 Working alone, make rough notes of any points that come to mind:

- Details observed through your senses
- Colours
- Comparisons
- Central idea (for example: seeing the daffodils is the centre of Dorothy's description).

5 Now turn your points into sentences and paragraphs. Dorothy writes in one long paragraph. You might prefer to structure your piece more clearly. Which tense will you write in? Dorothy is remembering, so she uses the past tense for verbs. If you want more drama and to seem to be reliving your experience, use the present tense.

6 When you have done a draft, check your piece for descriptive technique. Are your adjectives fresh and exact? Are your verbs bold enough? Have you used enough comparisons?

Review

Look again at the poem extract and the diary entry. Which is better as descriptive writing? Why?

Shakespeare's theatre

Aims

- To reconsider writing to explain.
- To look again at its technique.
- To write an outline explanation of the development of Shakespeare's theatre.

Starter session

In *Henry V* (1599) (Text 1), William Shakespeare (through his character, the Chorus) apologizes for the crudeness of his Company's stage presentation of the great story:

TEXT 1

HENRY V (extract)

'[…] But pardon, gentles all,
The flat unraised spirits that hath dared
On this unworthy scaffold to bring forth
So great an object. Can this cockpit hold
The vasty fields of France? Or may we cram
Within this wooden O the very casques
That did afright the air at Agincourt?.[…]'

Vocabulary

gentles – ladies and gentlemen

cockpit – small arena for cockfighting, a cruel gambling sport

vasty – huge

casques – helmets

afright – frighten

Agincourt – the great English battle victory over the French, October, 1415

- With a partner, discuss what the Chorus is saying about the problem of showing on stage a battle that involved thousands of men.

- What do the phrases 'unworthy scaffold', 'this cockpit' and 'wooden O' tell you about the nature of the theatre in Shakespeare's time? Make brief notes and then share them with the class.

Introduction

The rediscovery of the remains of the Elizabethan 'Rose' and 'Globe' theatres in the 1980s, and the opening of the reconstructed 'Globe' in 1996, created tremendous interest in the staging of Shakespeare's plays.

Here are some scattered notes about the subject, not in chronological order. Read them carefully.

a Women's parts were acted by boys. No woman appeared on the stage until 1660.

b The first 'Globe' was burned down in 1613, when a stage cannon shot blazing material onto the thatched roof.

c Actors formed professional Companies that played at particular theatres. Shakespeare's troupe was sponsored by Queen Elizabeth's Lord Chamberlain and then by King James I himself.

d Medieval religious plays were acted in churches or on rough stages erected in the market-place.

e The first purpose-built theatre was the 'Theatre' (1576) in Shoreditch, just north of the London city wall. The 'Curtain' was built nearby. Theatres were considered dangerous by the city authorities and were forbidden inside the City itself.

f Plays were performed in the afternoon. There were no stage lights.

g Travelling groups of actors toured the country in the 1570s and 1580s. As a boy, Shakepeare saw them act at Stratford-upon-Avon Guildhall.

h In the 1580s and 1590s, new theatres sprang up in Southwark on the south bank of the Thames near London Bridge. These included the 'Rose', the 'Swan' and the 'Globe', all of them round, thatched buildings with open tops.

i There was little realistic stage scenery. There were, however, colourful props and fancy costumes.

j Shakespeare's later plays were acted indoors at the small 'Blackfriars' theatre. Because it was indoors, more spectacular lighting and special effects could be employed.

k Ordinary working people paid a little to stand to watch plays. Others had seats in the galleries. The most expensive seats were stools on or near the stage itself.

l Up to 1576, travelling actors used to perform in the yards of City inns. The inn galleries around the yards allowed spectators to see the stage. The inn-yard gave a pattern for the theatre itself.

m In 1643, the second 'Globe' was destroyed by the Puritans, who hated theatre.

n Plague sometimes closed the theatres for a year at a time in the 1590s.

With a partner, put these points in order, by listing the letters. Remember that order is important in explanation. Discuss with your partner which of these ideas are most interesting or striking.

Development

You are going to write a short explanatory guide (two sides of A4 paper) about the development of theatre, from a cart in the market-place to the destruction of the second 'Globe'. The audience is next year's Year 9 pupils. Like all such explanatory writing, it should be:

● Clear
● In logical order
● Chronological
● Illustrated by detail, examples and dates.

1 Working alone, make a plan of the points that you are going to include. The notes in the Introduction will be useful but simplify and use your own words.

2 When you are happy with your note selection, turn them into short paragraphs: bullet points would be a good format.

3 Some pictures from books or from the Internet would be a valuable addition. Presentation is going to be important in your final draft: some of your audience may never have done Shakespeare before and may need to be won over!

Review

Think about a modern theatre. How does it differ from one in Shakespeare's times? Are there any similarities? Make quick notes and then put your ideas to the class.

Speech! Speech!

Aims

- To look again at persuasive writing.
- To study a persuasive speech in Shakespeare's *Julius Caesar*.
- To compose a speech using rhetorical devices and effects.

Starter session

Think of famous leaders in the twentieth and twenty-first centuries celebrated for making speeches. Can you think of any particular speeches? What were they about? Why were such speeches made? Put up your hands and tell the class what you know.

Great speeches are based on effects of persuasive language worked out long ago in ancient Greece and Rome. Politicians learn these 'rhetorical devices' in their public speaking training. Listen to any important speech by an American President and you can clearly hear 'rhetoric' at work.

Introduction

William Shakespeare (1564–1616) was almost certainly trained in rhetoric and he uses it with wonderful skill in his plays and poems.

In his Roman tragedy *Julius Caesar* (1599), Shakespeare wrote some of his most brilliant persuasive speeches. His drama was based on real events: the assassination of Julius Caesar, the Roman dictator, on 15 March 44BC. Romans were very proud of their Republic, a system of government with a careful balance of power. But with the threat of Caesar becoming King, a group of conspirators, including his great friend Brutus, decide to kill him. At Caesar's funeral, Brutus and Mark Antony, another close friend of Caesar who was not in the conspiracy, make speeches. Antony speaks second. He has a difficult task. He speaks to a hostile crowd in the square outside the Roman Parliament where Caesar was stabbed to death.

Vocabulary

lend me your ears – listen to me

interred – buried

they – the conspirators

thrice – thre times

Lupercal – a Roman festival

JULIUS CAESER (extract)

Antony

Friends, Romans, countrymen, lend me your ears.
I come to bury Caesar, not to praise him.
The evil that men do lives after them;
The good is oft interred with their bones:
So let it be with Caesar. The noble Brutus
Hath told you Caesar was ambitious.
If it were so, it was a grievous fault,
And grievously hath Caesar answered it.
Here, under leave of Brutus, and the rest,
For Brutus is an honourable man,
So are they all, all honourable men
Come I to speak in Caesar's funeral.
He was my friend, faithful, and just to me;
But Brutus says he was ambitious,
And Brutus is an honourable man.
He hath brought many captives home to Rome,
Whose ransoms did the general coffers fill:
Did this in Caesar seem ambitious?
When that the poor have cried, Caesar hath wept:
Ambition should be made of sterner stuff,
Yet Brutus says he was ambitious,
And Brutus is an honourable man.
You all did see that on the Lupercal
I thrice presented him a kingly crown,
Which he did thrice refuse. Was this ambition?
Yet Brutus says he was ambitious,
And sure he is an honourable man.
I speak not to disprove what Brutus spoke,
But here I am to speak what I do know.
You all did love him once, not without cause;
What cause withholds you then to mourn for him?
O judgement, thou art fled to brutish beasts,
And men have lost their reason! Bear with me,
My heart is in the coffin there with Caesar,
And I must pause, till it come back to me.

(III, 2, 73–107)

Antony then shows the crowd Caesar's cloak or mantle, full of knife gashes, that covers his dead body.

JULIUS CAESER (extract)

Antony
If you have tears, prepare to shed them now.
You all do know this mantle. I remember
The first time ever Caesar put it on.
Twas on a summer's evening in his tent,
That day he overcame the Nervii.
Look, in this place ran Cassius' dagger through;
See what a rent the envious Casca made;
Through this, the well-beloved Brutus stabbed,
And, as he plucked his cursèd steel away,
Mark how the blood of Caesar followed it,
As rushing out of doors, to be resolved
If Brutus so unkindly knocked, or no;
For Brutus, as you know, was Caesar's angel.
Judge, O you gods, how dearly Caesar loved him!
This was the most unkindest cut of all;
For when the noble Caesar saw him stab,
Ingratitude, more strong than traitors' arms,
Quite vanquished him. Then burst his mighty heart,
And in his mantle muffling up his face,
Even at the base of Pompey's statue,
Which all the while ran blood, great Caesar fell.
O what a fall was there, my countrymen!
Then I, and you, and all of us fell down,
Whilst bloody treason flourished over us.
O now you weep, and I perceive you felt
The dint of pity. These are gracious drops.
Kind souls, what weep you, when you but behold
Our Caesar's vesture wounded? Look you here!
Here is himself, marred, as you see, with traitors.

(III, 2, 169–97)

Vocabulary

Nervii – a German tribe

Cassius/Casca – other conspirators

Pompey – Caesar's dead rival for power

statua – statue

marred – spoiled

Development

1 Read this two-part speech at least twice.

2 Then, with a partner, look at the content of the speech.

- Look at the opening appeal for sympathy.
- 'Honourable' is a very strong word, and is Brutus's best quality. How does Antony degrade this word? Where does he finally destroy it?

- Antony wants to show that Caesar was not an ambitious man. What four reasons does he provide as evidence?
- How does Antony deal with Caesar's worst point: his desire to be King?

3 Now look at the rhetorical devices and persuasive language. Where do you find:

- Repetition
- Points leading to a climax
- Particular examples
- Exaggerated adjectives
- Emotive words and sentences.
- Rhetorical questions (that expect a certain answer)
- Well-chosen adjectives
- Comparisons

4 Think about Brutus's speech which came before Antony's. <u>Do not look it up in the play</u>. You are going to try writing it yourself. Here are some points from the speech to use in your own:

- Brutus loved Caesar as a friend.
- He loved Rome more.
- Caesar wanted to be King.
- Romans hated the one-man rule of a King.
- They were proud of being free men.
- They did not want to be slaves.
- Brutus was sad about Caesar's death.
- He was happy about his successes.
- He admired his courage.
- He hated his ambition to be King.
- He had to die because he was a threat to Roman freedom.

5 Try to include these ways of writing to persuade:

- appeal for sympathy
- repetition
- contrasted statements
- rhetorical questions
- points leading to a climax
- final appeal to the crowd.

6 After preparing your notes as a flow chart, write your piece as one longish paragraph.

7 When you revise and proofread your draft, check that its points are clear, that it is appealing, and varied in its style.

Review

Look again at Antony's speech. Which parts of it are most effective as persuasion? How exactly does the language contribute to this? Share your ideas with the class.

Arguments and counter-arguments

Aims

- To look again at writing arguments.
- To think about argument and counter-argument.
- To write a letter about the benefits of television.

Starter session

The two great general aims of broadcasting in Britain are:
- To inform
- To entertain.

Think about your own television viewing. Jot down under the two headings the names of three programmes that currently keep you informed or entertained.

Then look back over previous years. What are your all-time favourite information and entertainment programmes (one of each)? Tell the class about your various conclusions.

Introduction

Sometimes we see television as a wonder that can show us sunset on Mars or a World Cup goal being scored on the other side of the earth. Sometimes, by contrast, it can seem a blight on life, an electronic child-minder that kills children's creativity with silly cartoons, or wastes hours of adults' time on 'soaps' or hospital dramas.

- Read this letter to a magazine. It is a protest against the destructive effects of television.

Dear editor,

It was a black day for the human race, when, in 1926, John Logie Baird, the Scottish inventor, transmitted the first effective television image (of a doll's head) from one room to another.

This invention was to change people from infinitely varied, creative individuals into passive, almost identical sitters-in-chairs spending hours of their precious lives staring at a glowing screen. I'm going to suggest some convincing reasons why television is so bad for us.

Firstly, they say it informs us. There is indeed lots of news but it's mostly spectacular disasters, a war somewhere, scandal, doom and gloom. Do we really <u>understand</u> more about the world? It tells us so much about the supposed faults of politicians that many of us in the Western world no longer bother to vote. Is this 'being informed'?

Secondly, there is education from the small screen. We enjoy programmes about science, history or the natural world while we watch them but they pass so quickly that we forget them too easily. A book is much better, isn't it? You can go back to re-read or linger over an illustration. Television in schools is an amusing extra but we really <u>learn</u> from text books!

Thirdly, does television entertain us? Comedy programmes often contain crude ideas and bad language that have a bad effect on children and teenagers. 'Soaps' are just electronic wallpaper. <u>Neighbours</u>, <u>Coronation Street</u>, <u>EastEnders</u>: they are all the same with unrealistic people doing unrealistic things day after day. Give them up! Go for a walk! Paint a picture! Dig the garden! Do anything but watch 'soaps'!

Finally, there is televised sport. It's surely over-rated. If we <u>did</u> sports rather than simply watch them, we would be better physically (because of the exercise) and mentally (because of the achievement). All sports look too easy on television: it's different running on that pitch, hitting that ball, or straining to win that race. Television also makes sportsmen too highly paid and excessively important in our society. What is a footballer compared to a great musician, a leading scientist or a heart surgeon? Television has distorted our values!

To sum up: television spies on us in the streets; it makes us buy things we do not need; it damages our precious eyes; and above all, it makes us all the same. Switch it off! Get a life!

Yours faithfully,
'Angry' of Nottingham

With a partner, think again about features of writing to argue:

- Key points
- Introduction
- Rhetorical questions
- List leading to a climax
- Imperatives.

- Clear paragraphs
- Conclusion
- Repetition
- Slogans

- Find examples of these in the letter. Now make a list of the key themes of each paragraph.

For example:

> Television as entertainment
> a) comedy shows
> b) 'soaps'

Development

1 Now, let's think of a counter-argument to the letter above. You think television is a wonderful invention that has enriched human life. You write a letter answering 'Angry' of Nottingham. Try to respond to each one of the points you noted from the letter.

> I disagree with 'Angry's' point about comedy programmes. Many shows, like **'Dad's Army'**, are entirely innocent fun and are loved by huge audiences. They give particular comfort to the elderly and lonely.'

2 'Angry' has four main paragraphs with an introduction and conclusion. Give your answer a similar pattern. Try to use some of the 'rhetorical devices' noted above to give your argument more flair and conviction.

3 When you have finished a draft, check it point by point against 'Angry's' letter to see if you have mounted a convincing counter-argument.

Review

What, to you, is the single best feature of television? And what is the worst? Make quick notes and discuss your observations with the class.

The rules of the road

Aims

- To reconsider writing to advise.
- To look again at the technique, style and audience of this writing.
- To write advice about road safety.

Starter session

Think about your use of roads as a pedestrian, a cyclist, or in a bus or car.

a Some of these uses are controlled by law: you must do this or that.

b Some are only controlled by advice, given to you at school or by the government through the Highway Code.

With a partner, see how many points you can think of relating first to a) and then to b). Make a rough list.

Introduction

We all use the roads every day. The huge number of vehicles means that the roads are a dangerous environment, especially for children and young people.

As you have probably found in your Starter session, very few aspects of your road use are actually covered by law. Much depends on advice.

1 Remind yourself of features of advice writing:

- **Clarity**: straightforward wording and layout
- **Order**: one point following logically from another
- **Sense of audience**: tone and language suitable for intended readers
- **Modal verbs**: helping verbs (auxiliaries) attached to main verbs. They express obligation, permission, prohibition and condition. Examples: can, might, may, should, ought to, would, will, have to, etc
- **Imperative verbs**: they give commands. Examples: Do this now! Stop at the yellow line.

2 Now read this page from a **'Young Person's Highway Code'** (Text 1). This section tells you how to behave in cars. The points are not in order.

GOING IN CARS

1 Get in and out using the door nearer to the pavement.

2 You should behave quietly as you travel. You should not distract the driver.

3 Be very careful with electric windows.

4 If you have animals with you, control them carefully.

5 Do not touch the door handle while the car is moving.

6 Get out only when you are told to do so.

7 Check that your door is firmly closed.

8 Always wear your seat-belt in the front or the back of the car.

9 You must not lean out of or wave from the window.

10 Make sure that you do not block the driver's rear-view mirror. It is important that the driver sees the traffic behind.

11 Never throw things from the window.

3 With a partner, read over this advice. Then work through these questions.

- In which order of importance would you place the points?
- Is it clear enough? Are there any words unsuitable for a young audience? Could some sentences be shorter?
- Why are there more modal than imperative verbs?
- Are any points unnecessary?

Development

1 Write an advice sheet for 8–12 year olds about what to do as a pedestrian. It should be concise (one side of A4 paper) and very clear. It has got to be useful: far too many children are killed or injured on the roads each year.

There are many points to include, but you are concentrating on the most important. Working alone, make preparation notes. Here are some suggestions to get you started:

- Wearing light-coloured or fluorescent clothing at night
- Keeping to the pavement
- The Green Cross Code
- Crossing at traffic lights: the green man
- Using crossing patrols
- Crossing after getting off the bus
- Using traffic islands
- Helping younger children
- Zebra crossings
- Playing ball near the road
- Walking your dog
- Crossing through parked vehicles
- Using subways or footbridges
- Crossing at bends, junctions or on the brow of a hill
- Understanding road signs.

2 Now pick six to eight points that you consider important. Make each into a short paragraph of a few sentences. Keep the sentences short and the words simple. Bullets or numbers might be appropriate. Remember your modal and imperative verbs. Some illustration/diagrams might help. Set out the final draft very clearly.

Review

If you were discussing safety in the home, which dangers would deserve commands, and which advice? Share your thoughts with the class.

A Shakespearean sonnet

Aims

- To look again at writing to analyse.
- To reconsider techniques of analytical writing.
- To write a short analysis of a Shakespeare sonnet.

Starter session

Think again about different forms of poetry. Here are some examples:

- Elegy
- Lyric
- Narrative
- Ballad
- Haiku

Tell the class about anything you remember about what these forms of poetry do and how they are written.

Introduction

The **sonnet** has been a favourite poetic form in English literature from writers in Tudor times right up to contemporary authors like Seamus Heaney. The sonnet was invented in Italy in the late Middle Ages. It can be about anything that we humans are concerned about: its favourite subjects are people, war, love, religion, time and the natural world.

Sonnets have a particular shape and pattern. See if you can work these out, or remind yourself of what you know already, by looking at this sonnet by Thomas Hardy (1840–1928). It describes how Hardy's parents first fell in love in a Dorset village church, where his father, a stonemason, played the violin in the small church orchestra.

1 Read Text 1 together as a class.

TEXT **1**

A CHURCH ROMANCE

She turned in the high pew, until her sight
Swept the west gallery, and caught its row
Of music-men with viol, book and bow
Against the sinking sad tower-window light.
She turned again; and in her pride's despite
One strenuous viol's inspirer seemed to throw
A message from his string to her below,
Which said: 'I claim thee as my own forthright!'
Thus their hearts' bond began, in due time signed.
And long years thence, when Age had scared Romance,
At some old attitude of his or glance
That gallery scene would break upon her mind,
With him as minstrel, ardent, young, and trim,
Bowing 'New Sabbath' or 'Mount Ephraim'.

> ## Vocabulary
> *viol* – violin
> *New Sabbath/Mount Ephraim* – hymn tunes

2 With a partner, count the lines. Sonnets almost always have this number. Now look at the line endings and work out the rhyme scheme. Call the first rhyme A, the second B and so on. Write down the pattern.

Each line has ten syllables (or separate sounds) in it. They are arranged in a pattern with five stressed (or heavier) sounds, and five unstressed (lighter) sounds. This pattern is called 'pentameter' meter. You mark the stressed **(/)** and the unstressed **(u)**. The pentameter is therefore:

u / u / u / u / u /

3 Look at the first four lines and work out how the pattern fits them. Copy them and fill in the stress marks over the appropriate syllables.

Sonnets often divide into sections. This has an eight line section (*octet*) and a six line section (*sestet*). Here the octet is about the young couple's first expression of love. The sestet shows them years later, looking back on their meeting.

4 What is the **theme** (or general idea) of this sonnet?

Development

Now you have revised sonnet form, you can try a written analysis of a Shakespeare sonnet.

William Shakespeare wrote 154 sonnets, collected and published (probably against his wishes) in 1609. He probably wrote most of these 'sugared sonnets' privately for friends in the 1590s. Luckily for us, one of these friends decided to put them into print. Shakespeare's great themes are love and time.

1 As a class, read Text 2:

TEXT **2**

SONNET 73

That time of year thou mayst in me behold
When yellow leaves, or none, or few, do hang
Upon those boughs which shake against the cold,
Bare ruined choirs where late the sweet birds sang.
In me thou seest the twilight of such day
As after sunset fadeth in the west,
Which by and by black night doth take away,
Death's second self that seals up all in rest.
In me thou seest the glowing of such fire
That on the ashes of his youth doth lie,
As on the deathbed whereon it must expire,
Consumed with that which it was nourished by.
This thou perceiv'st, which makes thy love more strong,
To love that well which thou must leave ere long.

Vocabulary

behold – see
choirs – church ruins
birds – choirboys
Death's second self – sleep
leave – give up

The narrator, who may or may not be Shakespeare, is older than his lover. He wants to show that this may not be a problem: it could add intensity to their relationship.

2 You are going to write an analysis of this poem, aimed at people of your own age who do not know about Shakespeare's sonnets. Your analysis should put across the interest and power of the poem.

Here are some criteria to make a structure for your piece:

- Rhyme scheme
- The structure (four lines rhymed together = quartet; two line rhymed together = couplet)
- The pentameter rhythm
- The three comparisons describing the narrator
- The message of the last two lines
- What you personally find beautiful or interesting in the poem.

3 Remember that analysis means looking closely at the details: what exactly, for example, does 'bare ruined choirs' mean? Work on these preparation notes with a partner. You are going to need close references and quotations to illustrate your points: choose some from the poem.

4 Then, working alone, turn your points into paragraphs. A short **introduction** (about Shakespeare's sonnet writing) and a **conclusion** (about your personal reactions) would complete the analysis. Check the quotation marks carefully in your finished piece.

Review

Shakespeare's sonnets are famous for their wonderful imagery (use of comparisons). What is being compared to what in these lines?

Share your ideas with the class.

'Like as the waves make towards the pebbled shore,
So do our minutes hasten to their end.'
(Sonnet 60)

'When forty winters shall besiege thy brow,
And dig deep in thy beauty's field.'
(Sonnet 2)

'Full many a glorious morning have I seen
Flatter the mountain tops with sovereign eye,
Kissing with golden face the meadows green,
Gilding pale streams with heavenly alchemy.'
(Sonnet 33)

Reviewing a play

Aims

- To remind ourselves of the purpose of writing to review.
- To look again at techniques of reviewing.
- To write a review based on a Shakespeare play.

Starter session

How many Shakespeare plays can you think of? Share your ideas with the rest of the class and make a class list.

The plays are usually divided into tragedies, comedies and histories. What do these terms mean? Can you each write three example titles under the three headings?

Introduction

In Year 8, we looked at ways to review a piece of prose fiction and we saw how aspects of the book can give us a structure for a review:

- Brief summary
- Character
- Setting in time and place.

To consider a play, you would include these points together with other features typical of drama:

- **Conflict**. The characters on the stage struggle with each other or against their own feelings
- **Contrast**. A clash of opposites makes for good drama: old and young; rich and poor; serious and comic; peace and war, for example
- **Empathy**. We identify so strongly with characters on the stage that we almost become these people and share their feelings.

Think of a Shakespeare play that you know well, perhaps your SAT set play, *Macbeth, Twelfth Night* or *Henry V*.

1 With a partner, identify scenes of conflict and contrast in these plays.

2 With which characters do you share strong feelings of empathy?

Development

Now we are going to write a review of a scene or episode from a Shakespeare play.

Our audience is students of your own age who do not know this play. Remember that the purpose of a review is often to create interest and that some people are suspicious of Shakespeare, so you will need to be very positive and stimulating in what you say.

1 You are going to need an opening paragraph that offers a very brief outline of the play's general story and setting.

Example:

> Henry V is one of Shakepeare's history plays. People in Shakespeare's time looked back on Henry as a great King, who had united England after years of civil war by declaring war on France. The heart of the play is the drama surrounding the English victory over the French at Agincourt in October 1415. By Henry's brilliant leadership, a small English army defeats a huge French force. Henry's marriage to a French princess temporarily ends the war and closes the play.

2 Working alone, make a structure for your other paragraphs. Start with a list of numbered points like these:

- What is the **'story'** of this scene?
- **Where and when** does your scene take place?
- Who are the main **characters** and, briefly, what are they like?
- What are the **exciting, tragic or comic aspects** of this scene?
- Where do you see **conflict and contrast**? (Don't forget that a character can be in conflict with himself, like Macbeth before his murder of King Duncan.)
- **Language**: which words and lines do you find interesting or exciting? Shakespeare's use of **imagery** (comparisons) is often particularly memorable.
- Your conclusion might deal with your **personal reactions** to the drama. Which parts did you enjoy?

4 Now move on from your outline. Look over your scene and find some quotations to illustrate it. It is a good idea to use them in a drama review. You can do it in two ways:

- **Explicit quotation**

  This is where you make a point followed by your quotation. If it is less than two lines long, it can go on the same line as your writing. If the quotation does not fit into the structure of your sentence, it should be introduced by a colon, with quotation marks to start and finish it.

  For example:

  > Macbeth shows feelings of remorse and guilt after killing King Duncan: 'Wake Duncan with thy knocking: I would thou couldst!'

- **Embedded quotation**

  Sometimes you can show considerable skill by making the quotation part of your sentence. If you do, you do not need to introduce it with a colon, but you should still use quotation marks:

  For example:

  > When trying to decipher what he is seeing in the dagger scene, Macbeth initially wonders if it is the result of his 'heat-oppressed brain'.

5 When you have prepared your outline, turn the points into complete paragraphs. Do not write too much: two sides of A4 paper at most. Make your review lively and enthusiastic: you want to persuade your audience that Shakespeare is exciting! When you check over the final draft, look carefully at the spellings of names and places, and at the punctuation of your quotations.

Review

Shakespeare's plays were intended to be **seen**, not just read. What film, TV or video versions of Shakespeare have you seen? What does seeing a scene add to its drama? Think of specific examples that you remember and tell the class your ideas about them.